# BERTIE AND ME

# Bertie and Me

## Growing Up on a Nebraska Sandhill Ranch in the Early 1900's

Billie Lee Snyder Thornburg

**101**

## THE OLD HUNDRED AND ONE PRESS
North Platte, Nebraska

Published by The Old 101 Press
2202 Leota Drive
North Platte, NE 69101


Printed in the United States of America


Cover Design by Kay and Ryan Cooper
Book Design by Kai Crozer
Edited by Ann Milton


Library of Congress Control Number:  2002111246
Thornburg, Billie Lee Snyder
Bertie and Me / by Billie Lee Snyder Thornburg
p. cm.
Summary: Tells about kids growing up on a ranch in the sandhills of Nebraska from 1912 to 1927.
ISBN 0-9721613-0-9

# Dedication

To my sister Bertie who helped me live this life
and
To all the Sandhill kids who helped us have our fun --
the Tregos, the Huffmans, the Cliffords, the Van Meters,
the Melvins, the Pinkertons, the Daleys, the Quinns,
the Tuckers, the Winters and the Pophams

## A Word From Bertie

*"I don't care what Bill says. She did, too, tell me
to hit that teacher on the head
with the monkey wrench."*

# Acknowledgements

I wish to thank Ann Milton who insisted I write these stories, then edited the entire book. She also became my agent, public relations manager and very good friend. At times she got downright bossy. Thank you, Ann.

To all the members of our writing group who laughed at my stories as I read them, then encouraged me to write another.

To Helen Petitt Mitchel who helped me with the Helping Hand Club stories.

To Kai Crozer who came from Apache Junction, Arizona to design the layout.

To my nephew, Jim Snyder, and his wife, Joyce, who still live on the Ten Bar Ranch where these stories took place. Thank you, Jim and Joyce, for drawing a great sandhills map.

To Kay Cooper and her son Ryan, the North Platte artists who did the beautiful cover.

Also to my husband, Bob, who sat in his chair and kept from talking as I worked, and to Charlie, my white Goffens' cockatoo who perched on my shoulder repeating over and over, "Don't give up, Billie. Don't give up, Billie," as I sat at my computer.

# Foreword

Many of us recall, and dwell, on incidents that have occurred in the past, the major part--childhood reflections. The tendency to keep them within ourselves too often prevails. Present and future generations are denied the knowledge and worth that these experiences provide.

Billie Snyder Thornburg emphasizes family. She delights in leisurely telling of incidents that constituted daily routine in the maintenance of a pioneer ranch home.

I was to become knowledgeable of this versatiole family after my beginning in a sod house, about twelve miles west of the Snyder's, near the post office/store of Flats.

The years would prove their's a talented family from the start to the end. The father, Albert Benton Snyder, an early-day cowboy, colorful in every respect, and becoming an established cattle rancher in the Nebraska Sandhills; the mother, Grace, besides a fine homemaker, was a champion quilt maker; Nellie Irene, a noted writer and author of "Call of the Range," the popular Nebraska cattle history book (1966); Miles William, who grew up in ranching but also possessed a writing vein (his poem on the Model T Ford is a classic); Beulah Lee "Billie," author of this fascinating book; and Flora Alberta "Bertie," with many friends among the Nebraska Cow-Belles and 1968-69 president of the state-wide auxiliary of the Nebraska Stock Growers Association.

Much of Billie's writing is emotional to me, having encountered some of the same situations, however without the sibling relationship until age thirteen. The author, her sisters and brother comprised the eagerness that often characterizes families.

Billie's family helped make history and here she is recording it. She puts this affable family in the perspective that it deserves. With the publication of this book, Billie Snyder Thornburg earns her niche in family traditions.

--Robert M. Howard

# Foreword

*It is a world and a time a few can remember and most cannot imagine. Billie Thornburg writes of children growing up on a Sandhills ranch between 1912 and 1927. It was a hard life but a close family. Children were expected to work and did. Billie drove a stacker team in the hay field when she was six. "If it was for fun and cost money, we didn't get it or do it... But we made our own fun and the folks were always there."*

*These are plain stories, plainly written and with the wry humor of a 90-year-old woman who never completely outgrew her childhood. There is a laugh or a chuckle in every chapter.*

*Billie Lee Snyder Thornburg is a younger sister of the late Nellie Snyder Yost, whose earlier books about their father (Pinnacle Jake) and their mother (No Time on My Hands) launched a distinguished writing career. But this is a distinctly different view of life on the Snyder ranch.*

*It is also a fascinating look at how people lived in one part of the country before the 20th Century changed everything for all of us.*

*-- Keith Blackledge*
*Editor Emeritus, North Platte Telegraph*

# CONTENTS

# The Bert Snyder Ranch vicinity in McPherson County, Nebraska – Early 1900's

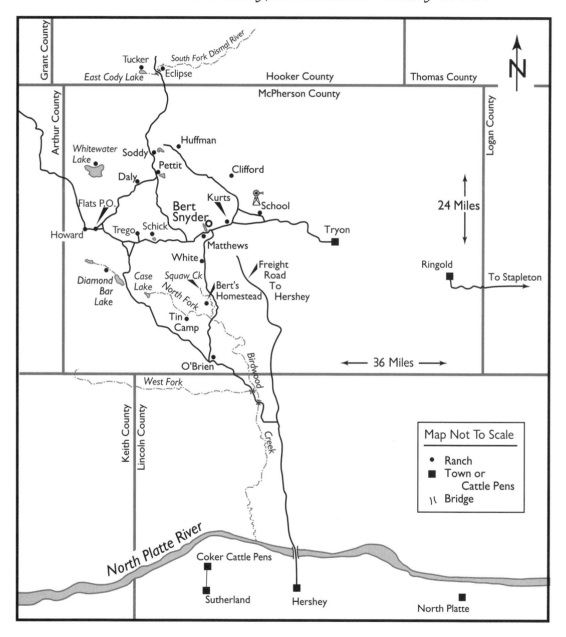

Grant County

Tucker

South Fork Dismal River

East Cody Lake

Eclipse

Hooker County

Thomas County

N

McPherson County

Arthur County

Logan County

Huffman

Whitewater Lake

Soddy

Pettit

Clifford

Daly

Flats P.O.

Bert Snyder

Kurts

School

24 Miles

Howard

Trego

Schick

Tryon

Matthews

White

Ringold

Freight Road To Hershey

To Stapleton

Diamond Bar Lake

Case Lake

Squaw Ck

North Fork

Bert's Homestead

Tin Camp

36 Miles

O'Brien

Birdwood

West Fork

Keith County

Lincoln County

Creek

**Map Not To Scale**

• Ranch
■ Town or Cattle Pens
)\ Bridge

North Platte River

Coker Cattle Pens

Sutherland

Hershey

North Platte

*Dad on Nibs in their older years.*
*Notice the ranch trees are much taller.*

*Mama on Chief with the hayrack*
*in the background.*

*Our ranch house in winter.*

*Rounding up the cattle.*

*My brother, Miles, ready to rope at branding.*

*My sister Nellie*

*Billie on Chief and Bertie on Roanie giving the horses a drink.*

*And then there was Bird, the colt that was an accident. I loved her and had so much fun and felt she belonged to me. I don't know why I named her Bird. This is my favorite picture!*

*Mama tried hard to make a lady out of Bertie!*

*2002*
*The result of hard living.*
*Bertie Snyder Elfeldt on the left and Billie Lee Snyder Thornburg on the right.*

## Chapter One

# OUR FAMILY

This story takes place in the sandhills of Nebraska on the Ten-Bar Ranch twelve miles west of Tryon. We were six: Dad, Mama, Nellie the oldest, Miles, fifteen months younger, me (Billie or Bill), five years and six months younger than Miles, and Bertie, two years younger than I.

Mama and Dad were of the old school: teach the kids to work and don't spoil them with too much attention or too many toys. If it was for fun and cost money, we didn't get it or do it. After all, we had that mortgage on the ranch to pay off and that was up to the whole family. But we made our own fun and the folks were always there.

Dad might be out on horseback a few miles from the house, but he would be home at mealtime. Sometimes he was gone from early morning to late afternoon. Those were the times Bertie and I climbed up on the barn to watch in the direction he would come riding in out of the hills. We missed him.

Mama was mostly in the house or nearby. If Dad or Miles came into the kitchen to get a drink of water and did not see Mama, the question would be, "Where's Mom?"

Whichever one of us was in the kitchen would tell where Mom was and ask, "Did you want her?" The answer was nearly always, "No, I just wondered where she was."

When one of us was gone overnight, a quiet, sad family was left behind.

*Nellie, Mama, Dad, Billie sucking her thumb, and Miles with their 1910 Ford.*
*Dad liked the top down but it irritated Mama.*

Nellie, who had a crooked back, could not ride horseback the five miles to school. She spent the winters in town going to school. She also spent many months in an orthopedic hospital in Lincoln where they tried to correct her crooked back. The times she was in the hospital she was gone from home even during the summer.

I recall Nellie being home once when I was very young and small. She and I were in the bathtub. She was wearing a heavy body cast that went from her hips to her armpits. She could only kneel in the tub. She couldn't get water up under the cast.

The bathtub was a real enameled clawfoot tub. It sat in a five-by-six-foot room that had an open doorway partitioned off from the kitchen by a curtain. We were very proud of that bathtub.

In order to take a bath, we pumped lots of water and heated it on the kitchen range in pans, buckets and the teakettle. When the water got hot enough, we carried it and poured it into that pretty tub. If the water in the tub was too hot, we pumped and poured in enough cold water to get it just right. After a wonderful bath in that tub we just pulled the plug and the water drained right outdoors on the grass. What a convenience. Those baths were lots of fun and could take most of an afternoon.

When it came time for Nellie to leave, whether to go back to the hospital or back to town to school, it was a very sad time for the whole family. The ranch seemed so empty without her. The few times she was home, she was treated like company.

Bertie and I loved it when Nellie came home for visits. Each evening she would put her book down and come upstairs with us at our bedtime and tell us two stories. She also had much else to tell us, things she learned while she was away. She

*Miles and Nellie*

*Nellie at the lake trying to get on Dina*

would tell us how things were different in town than on the ranch.

One thing that sticks in my mind was her telling us about basketball. She described how it was played. I told the kids at our school there was a wonderful new game called basketball. I tried to tell them how to play it, but I couldn't remember how it went. All I could think of was all the yelling they did. So I told the kids about that. One smart kid asked me how you could tell who won. I said, "The ones who yell the loudest win the game."

For a few days we played basketball in our school, yelling back and forth trying to see who could yell the loudest.

Neither the treatments in the Lincoln hospital nor wearing the thick, heavy cast that looked like it was made of cement helped Nellie's crooked back. She never quite reached four feet eight inches in height. She never minded being short. If she saw a kiddie's tricycle handy she would climb aboard and go for a spin.

In later years when she was called on to speak at banquets, she would be asked to "please stand." She would, but no one saw her. She would again be asked to stand. At that point she would climb up on her chair. That always brought a laugh.

Being short didn't slow her down one bit. She was a regular buzz saw, always getting things done - whether they needed it or not.

*Miles hunting with Fannie*

Miles, the only boy, was always there and was a very good brother. He did everything he was told to do and did it right away.

I remember him in his older years say, "It seemed like every time I went to the house for a drink of water, Mom needed a tub of cow chips for the chip box." That was the only time in seventy years I heard him complain about anything.

Miles was so good to his two little sisters. He did tease us some, but he always did anything we asked of him.

In those days people peeled their apples before eating them. Bertie and I always took our apples to Miles to peel with his jackknife. Miles had a jackknife with two blades in it. One blade he used to peel our apples and the other he used for skinning muskrats, skunks and coyotes.

We also took our pencils to him to sharpen with that jackknife. I don't know which blade he used for sharpening our pencils. At school we used the pencil sharpener, but at home Miles did it for us.

I remember one of Mile's teases. I was trying to read and came to a word I didn't know so I asked Miles, "What does W-H-A-T spell?"

*Nellie, Billie and Bertie with some of Fannie's puppies.*

*Mama and Dad's wedding picture, taken in North Platte, NE, 1903.*

He said, "What," and so I asked him again. Again he said, "What."

So I asked the same question much louder and he still said, "What."

I turned and looked at him. He had a quiet grin on his face and a laughing look in his eyes. I knew then what the word was and also knew that I had been had.

Then there were we two little girls, Billie and Bertie. Most of my stories will be about us. We are the only ones still alive so no one can contradict us.

Things were different back then. I'll try to write it the way it was, starting back in 1912 and 1914, the years Bertie and I were born. We are now limping into the sunset at ages 88 and 90.

## Chapter Two

# BERTIE AND ME

Bertie and I were, and still are, just two years apart in age. Bertie was born on the ranch, May 2, 1914. When it was time, word was sent to Dr. Sadler in Hershey, thirty miles south. In 1914 one could not call a doctor for there were no telephones in the sandhills yet. Word was sent to the doctor via the neighbors between our place and Hershey. The message was: "Mrs. Bert Snyder on the Snyder Ranch thirty miles north is in labor and wants Dr. Sadler."

The neighbors who carried the message down directed the doctor back to our place. In the eleven years the family had been on the ranch no doctor had ever been up there.

As soon as Mama realized the baby was sure enough coming, Dad got on his fastest, strongest horse and hightailed it to the neighbor south to give him the message. Mr. White readied his best horse and rode to the next ranch. The rancher at the next ranch rode to the next until word reached someone near Hershey who had a telephone and could ring Dr. Sadler from their place.

There was no doubt but the thirty miles of ranchers would have Doc on his way as soon as possible. Neighbors looked out for each other up there. The pony express method lived on in the sandhills long after it was used to carry the mail coast to coast.

*Billie in the saddle, friend Gertrude Cooker from Sutherland in the middle and Bertie on the rear of gentle old Snip.*

It would take at least four hours for Doc to reach the ranch after he received the hurry-up call. He traveled by team and buggy. There were at least twenty-five barbed-wire gates to go through.

The doctor drove fast, gentle horses. When coming to a gate, he stopped the team, wrapped the reins around the buggy whip holder, got out of the buggy, opened the gate, pulled it back to the side of the road and said, "Giddup" to the horses. The horses walked slowly through the gate until he hollered, "Whoa." The team stopped and waited for the doctor to close the gate, get back in the buggy, unwind the reins and slap them on the rump. Then they were off on a fast trot. After all, Doc was on a house call and in a hurry.

Meanwhile back at the ranch, Bertie wanted to get the birth over with and she has done things her way ever since. A neighbor, Mrs. Loveall, was with Mama. She was capable of handling a birth. When they realized Bertie was not going to wait for the doctor, Dad got on another good horse and started south to head the doctor off.

It was common practice for a doctor to charge a dollar a mile for country house calls. There was no extra charge for the service, just a dollar a mile for the distance traveled. In cases like this when the need for the doctor was over before he arrived, he was stopped as soon as they could reach him. The bill was one dollar a mile for as far as he had traveled. He didn't charge for the trip back to town.

The doctors in those days were rugged characters, the same as the rest of the population. We don't know how far Dr. Sadler traveled that day, but Bertie did save her dad several dollars. She is a very conservative person to this day.

As I was writing this story, I kept thinking, "Boy, in cases of this kind, the folks could have surely used one of those storks they were always telling Bertie and me about."

Bertie thinks she was special to have been the only one of us four kids born at the ranch, born with no doctor present and named after our dad. The folks had wanted and expected a boy, but they still named her after Dad, Alberta for Albert, thus the nickname Bertie. I must admit I envy her just a little for all of this.

*Billie holding Buster and Bertie holding Towser. Mama always made us wear our hats when we went outside. Notice our hats on the ground.*

Bertie doesn't know what time she was born but I know the exact time of my birth. It was April 12, 1912 at 5:25 A.M. When I asked Mama what time I was born she said, "It was early in the morning. You got here in time for breakfast and haven't missed a meal since." Mama always put a funny twist to something if she could.

I was born in Grandpa McCance's sod house a few miles north of Cozad. Everything was ready and planned. Nothing dramatic there. There is no record of what either Bertie or I weighed at birth or how tall we were. They may not have weighed babies in those days. At least I'm sure the doctor didn't carry a scale of any kind with him on house calls.

Grandma McCance named me Beulah. As far back as I can remember I've hated that name. I like the name on other people, I just hate it for myself. Somewhere along the line the family started calling me Billie. I held on to the name of Billie and Beulah just faded away.

Sibling rivalry was very strong between Bertie and me. It started with her birth and got stronger as we grew older. We spent our kid years each trying to outdo the other. As I look back I wish so much we could change that part of our kidhood. It would have certainly made it easier for our mama.

Bertie and I desperately wanted a baby brother. We knew Mama was the only one in the family who had direct contact with the stork. We both pestered her with, "Will you please get us a baby brother?"

*Bertie and I were once baby material.*

Her answer was always, "I'll get you a baby brother if you'll quit fussing at each other for a year."

We would swear off fussing, but it would only be a few hours until we were at it again. Mama didn't intend to have any more babies and she knew Bertie and I would never quit trying to outdo each other.

At ages 88 and 90 we try to hold it down, but now and then it pops up. We now know to get off the subject, back up and talk around it. We do see each other often. We enjoy getting together and we always wind up talking over "Old Times."

We talk of our old squabbles and laugh at them. We don't always remember things the same so we argue as to which one of us is right.

## Chapter Three

# KIDS AT WORK

The big box telephone on the west wall of our living room gave a GENERAL RING, several long rings and several short rings in any order. A general ring was very important and meant for everyone on that country line to take down their receiver and listen in. It was like a newsbreak on television.

Mama rushed to the phone, took down the receiver and seemed to freeze as she listened. Then she gave her dramatic yell and hung up the receiver.

I was standing there watching her to find out what had happened. She turned to me and said, "Billie, run down in the meadow and tell Daddy, 'THE WAR IS OVER." It was the forenoon of November 11, 1918.

The First World War had just ended. The war that was to have ended all wars for all time.

We, our whole family, Daddy 46, Nellie 13, Miles 12, myself 6 and Bertie 4, had helped Mama worry about her brother Roy who had been in France on the front line for several months. So far Uncle Roy hadn't received a scratch, as far as we knew.

It was a half mile to where Daddy was working. I remember the trip well. I tried to run as much as I could.

The folks had said many times that things would be better when the war was over. Our big treat was bread and butter and sugar. Sugar was rationed and when we asked for a slice of bread (homemade), butter (homemade also) and sugar, we were reminded we had to go easy on the sugar. Sometimes we got it and sometimes we didn't. Now maybe Bertie and I could have more bread and butter and sugar.

When I reached Daddy and told him the war was over, he quit working and I rode in the wagon with him back to the house.

I was soon worried about next summer. Last summer Daddy had put me to driving stacker team when they stacked hay. Would I get to work in the hay field again?

The biggest and toughest job on a ranch is putting up hay to feed the cattle during the winter months. Every ranch had one or more hired men during the haying months, July and August. During the war the ranchers couldn't get hired help. The young men were all overseas helping fight the KAISER. Every member of the family who could drive a team of horses worked in the hayfield.

In our family there was Daddy, Mama and eleven-year-old Miles to do the work of four or five men. It helped to have a kid drive stacker team. Dad had me, even though I was a six-year-old girl, maybe a bit too young for the job.

I had felt very proud of myself going to the hay field with the grownups each afternoon. I must have passed as a hay-hand as Dad gave me a five-dollar bill at the end of haying. The next time I got to town I bought two doll buggies with my five dollars, one buggy for my four-year-old sister Bertie and one for myself.

*Billie with one of the doll buggies she bought with the money she earned driving the stacker team.*

*Mama with her favorite team of Jake and Geronimo hitched to the hay rake.*

Dad did allow me to work in the hay field the next summer and each summer after that but never paid me again. He may not have approved of what I spent the money for.

Daddy and Miles mowed hay during the forenoon hours. Mama, with the help of the girls, worked in the large garden plus had a meal on the table when Daddy and Miles came in from mowing.

After dinner Mama put on a pair of coveralls (a bold thing to do in those days) to go out and rake hay all afternoon. There was a small box fastened on Mama's rake in which she carried a gallon crock jug of drinking water. The jug was sewn up in several thicknesses of burlap from an old gunnysack. The burlap was soaked with water when the jug was filled and the evaporation kept the water cold all afternoon. Filling the jug or jugs to take to the hay field was always a kid's job.

Bertie was too young to leave alone. She rode all afternoon in the box on Mama's rig with her little legs wrapped around the wet water jug. She says she can smell the wet burlap yet when she thinks of that jug.

Bertie liked to ride facing the back of the rake and watch the snakes and frogs that got caught up in the rake teeth and rolled over and over with the hay until it was dumped. If she faced the front all she saw was the two horses' rumps with their tails switching flies or one lifting its tail and letting go with a steamy bunch of road apples.

It took three teams of horses to stack hay: one team on the rake to rake the hay into long windrows, one team on the sweep that went down the windrows gathering a load of hay on the wide fork, and one stacker team. The sweep fork pushed the load of hay on the stacker fork. The sweep then backed out and went for another load of hay while the stacker team was driven out to throw its load on the stack.

I remember that first time I went to the hayfield to drive the stacker team. I was feeling plenty big for my six years. I drove the horses straight ahead for thirty or forty yards, trying and hoping to drop the hay just where the man on the stack wanted it. If I went too far the load of hay fell on the ground behind the stack. If I stopped too soon, the hay dropped down in the stacker frame in front of the stack. Either one was very embarrassing, even heartbreaking for a six-year-old girl too old to cry and too young to cuss.

At times I did feel big enough and old enough to cuss and I said, "Gosh Darn," "Doggone" or "Oh Heck." If I said anything worse than that, I knew I would go to hell, or the Bad Place as we called it.

*Billie (age 7) driving the stacker team to stack the hay.*

*The sweep team after loading hay on the stacker. The stacker team
is to the rear on the right.*

The man on the stack with his pitchfork spread the hay even, trying to keep the sides straight. The stacks were about twelve or fourteen feet high. When we finished one stack, the stacker team was hooked on to the stacker and pulled to a new spot nearer the newly raked windrows.

When the stacker was moved, all I had to do was ride on the stacker platform or, if I was lucky, Dad would let me climb up on the ladder that went to the top and ride there. That was really fun.

Usually we could put up two stacks of hay in an afternoon if no thunder and lightning storm came up to run us in out of the hayfield. Some afternoons seemed very long and hot and a big black cloud coming up in the west looked so-o-o good. It meant that we might get to quit early and if it did rain, the weather would cool off.

We came in from the hayfields before sundown to do the chores and eat supper before dark. In 1918 the only lights we had were kerosene lamps and lanterns. With the nice long days during the summer there was no need to light a lamp. By nine o'clock, "summer bed time," there was still enough daylight mixed with the darkness to go to bed. We were all up shortly after daybreak the next morning. I've heard Daddy tell people it didn't take long to stay all night at our house.

After coming in from the hayfield, hot, tired horses were unhitched, unharnessed and turned out in the pasture to eat and rest until the next afternoon. Different teams were used on the mowing machines the next morning. The first thing the horses did after being turned out was go to the tank and get a long drink of water, then trot out to a bare spot and roll in the dust. That dust must have felt good to their sweaty hides. I always waited to see them do it. They looked like they were having fun.

We had seven or eight milk cows during the summer. Mama said she had to have plenty of milk, cream and butter to cook with. We always had lots of thick, heavy cream for our cereals, puddings and strawberries. Mama put milk or cream in most of our vegetables.

Miles loved cabbage boiled in milk. When he was an old man in his eighties I heard him mention how great cabbage boiled in milk tasted.

After we turned the horses out we had the cows to milk before supper. I tried to help but I wasn't a very strong milker yet. I had to milk in a gallon bucket where Daddy and Miles used a much bigger bucket. We each sat on a one-legged milk stool and held the bucket between our knees. We were on the right side of the cow back where the milk comes out. A milker milks as fast as he can with both hands. A good fast milker will have a couple of inches of foam in his bucket full of milk.

I tried hard to milk fast and squeeze hard enough to get a big stream of milk. The first time I got foam I hurried around to show it to everyone before it disappeared. I even ran to the house to show Mama and Nellie.

Four-year-old barefooted Bertie gathered the eggs and fed the chickens by scattering shelled corn on the ground around her. Sometimes the chickens mistook her little toe nails for corn and pecked her toes. She didn't like that but she did like the chickens and often carried a little yellow, fuzzy baby chicken around in her hands or her romper pocket.

Daddy had to get the two mowing machines ready to go back to the field the next morning. He had to sharpen a six-foot sickle for each mower. To do this he sat on the grindstone seat, the large stone wheel in front of him. He peddled like a bicycle to turn the grindstone wheel. On a little platform just above the wheel sat a gallon can with a nail hole at the bottom. The nail was left in the hole so the water

*Bertie and Billie in the hay mow door. The grindstone Dad sharpened the sickles with is in the foreground.*

just dripped on the stone, keeping the stone from getting too hot. These sickles were six feet long and each had twenty-five blades that had to be sharpened each evening.

After the chickens and eggs were taken care of, the machinery ready to go to the field the next morning, and the milking finished, we had the milk to run through the separator. We saved a couple of gallons of skimmed milk for the family to drink the next day. The milk was put in two-gallon pails with tight lids. The cream was put in another gallon pail with a tight lid.

In the summertime these were taken down to the windmill by the garden. There was a little shed built by the windmill. The pipe from the mill went into a box in the shed. There was a pipe at the other end of the box and the water flowed on out and into the tank from which Mama watered a large garden including a wonderful strawberry patch. The cream that was kept in the cool box really tasted good on the berries that came out of the strawberry patch.

The rest of the skimmed milk was carried out to the pigpen and poured in the trough. I don't know how pigs got fat on skimmed milk, but they did. This same procedure of milking and caring for the milk was repeated in the morning before breakfast before going to the hayfield.

When the chores were finished, we all went in to supper, another big meal eaten in the kitchen. The kitchen was a large room and it was hot. There were two outside doors, one on the north and one on the south. If a breeze came up from either of these directions, the room cooled off considerably. The hot nights made you appreciate the cool ones.

After supper we kids usually had a water fight. We each got something to carry water in, the bigger the better. There were two pumps, one on the north porch and one out in the yard. Those water fights were fun. Each kid pumped his own water and then tried to slip up on another kid and throw the water on him or her.

Sometimes Mama let us run through the kitchen, one kid going in one door trying to get away from the chasing kid. The kid in front had already thrown his bucket of water and had nothing to fight with until he could get back to a pump. There was always one or more other kids to worry about.

Mama let us run through the kitchen but we couldn't throw water while in the house. Mamma always told us when to stop. She had no doubt had all she could take at that point. When the water fight was over, we kids were all soaking wet and cooled off. Those old blue denim overalls were plenty heavy and soaked up lots of water and it all felt so good.

If there was any twilight left after Mama stopped the water fights, we played hide-n-seek, still in our wet clothes. The best place for that game was out around the barn and sheds.

Soon we'd hear a loud call from the house, "BEDTIME!"

Dad's voice was strong. He knew we kids heard. We all came unhid in a hurry and ran to the house. We didn't fool around on the way. We had to get to bed and be ready to get up in the morning when we heard Mama's voice calling, "Kiddies, time to get up." It was time to get ready for another day in the hayfield plus chores and fun.

This was more or less what a kid's day on a ranch during haying in the 1920's was like. I wish I'd known at the time what a good life it was.

## Chapter Four

# Mama Goes To Vote

This story takes place April 20th, 1920. I had just turned five years old.

Bertie and I were sitting on the top rail of our eight-foot high wooden corral fence. We were facing east and it was a beautiful early spring morning. The sun was warm in our faces. We were watching our Mama and Dad riding east along a three-strand barbed-wire fence. They were horseback and were on their way to vote in the primary election.

Women had just received the right to vote in Nebraska. Mama would be thirty-eight-years old in three days on April 23rd and was voting for the first time in her life. It was a very important day for her.

The women could not vote for all that the men could, and men and women had separate ballots. The women could only vote for the president and vice-president and a few others. There was the big issue of prohibition, and the women could vote on that, which frightened many men, including our dad.

I remember hearing Dad say in a cross voice, "If women get the vote, they'll vote whiskey out." He was right!

As I said, it was a very important, very happy day for Mama. We kids were proud and happy, too. Somehow we felt a part of it all. Mama dressed in her best riding habit and rode a gentle but high-spirited sorrel-colored horse named Jeff, a horse she loved and loved to ride. Mama always sat so straight and proud. We thought she was beautiful.

*Mama as she looked when she went to vote for the first time in 1920. Here she is wearing her beaver hat. Mama always wore a hat.*

Dad was dressed as usual, only he was wearing his good Stetson hat. I'm sure he shined his boots, too. He always shined his boots before he left the ranch. He had also shaved that morning. I loved to watch him shine his boots and shave.

The polling place was nine miles northeast of our ranch. It was a one-room country schoolhouse set out in the Sandhills, no other buildings in sight. The folks would cut through many pastures and open and close many barbed-wire gates to get there. They had to be on horseback, know where the gates were and know one hill from the other to do that.

If they went around by the road in their 1910 Ford, it would be twice as far with twice as many gates to open, drive through and close. The road had been made by  wagon tracks in the sand, up hills and down hills. Taking the road, one had a pretty good chance of getting stuck in the sand, having a flat tire or some other break down. Horseback was a much faster, surer, safer trip. The polls were only open so many hours and they had to vote.

By the time the folks reached the voting place, cast their secret vote, visited with the neighbors and rode home again, it was late in the afternoon. Missing dinner meant nothing when something had to be done. They did this knowing they would kill each other's vote. Maybe Mama knew Dad would go vote regardless, so she had to go, too. Maybe they felt it was their duty to vote. For some reason they never agreed not to ride that eighteen miles every election day and kill each other's vote.

The eighteen miles horseback was not so bad for the spring primary election, as it came in April. The fall general election in Nebraska was in November and could be very cold. Bertie says she remembers one time Mama came home from voting almost frozen.

I often think of the time Bertie and I watched the folks ride off to vote when I am riding down the street a few blocks to cast my secret vote. I'm in a nice warm car and have no gates to stop and open. I'm wondering if it's worth it. Will my vote make a difference?

Dad died in 1956. He was eighty-four years old. Mama lived to be one-hundred years and eight months. She died in 1982. I am 90 now and Bertie 88. We live only about a mile apart and often get together. We always talk over old times. We don't always remember things the same, but we remember the same on the great day that Mama and all the women in Nebraska were allowed the right to vote.

## Chapter Five

# BOSSING BERTIE

As I remember, Bertie did everything I told her to, the things I wanted to do but knew I would receive a good scolding or a little paddlin' if I did them. She could get by with most things as she was too young to know better.

There was a neighbor by the name of Mr. Lawyer who used to stop in at our place. He was a very nice old man. He had one short leg and walked with a big limp. He was at our house one day talking to Mama.

As he was walking across the kitchen floor, I called Bertie over and whispered in her ear to go show Mr. Lawyer how he walked. She got out in the middle of the kitchen and said, "Mr. Lawyer, this is how you walk," then she limped across the floor in an exaggerated limp with her little arms dangling in front of her.

It seemed to me she did a great job, but Mama was so embarrassed Bertie received a big scolding. Mama embarrassed too easy to my way of thinking.

I dreamed up the games Bertie and I would play and they always worked to my advantage.

One of our games was betting. I told Bertie we would bet on what would happen or how things would turn out. And we would bet favors, usually five at a time. Whoever lost the bet had to do five favors for the other.

I mostly originated the bets and, of course, won. I had poor little Bertie waiting on me hand and foot. Then I came upon the wonderful idea that as the last

*Billie, a neighbor with a fishing pole, and Bertie*

favor I would demand that she give me another five favors. I will never forget the look on her face when I told her that.

The next time I remember bossing Bertie (it was about this time that Bertie started telling Mama "to make Bill quit bossing me"), it was spring and the lakes had thawed out. Our flat-bottomed boat was pulled up on the shore just south of the garden, about two city blocks south of the house. I got the great idea to go out in the boat and catch some fish for supper.

Bertie and I took a couple of bamboo fishing poles that were all ready for fishing. They had lines, hooks and bobbers.

We went in the kitchen and got a hunk of bacon for bait. We took a nice sharp paring knife to cut the bait. We took all this  down, put it in the boat and put our little bulldog in with us.

We picked up the oars and shoved off. Nothing to it, and here the folks had told us never to go out in the boat alone.

After we pushed off from shore, the wind came up strong. It started the boat toward the middle of the lake. The folks had told us the water in the middle would be over our heads. Neither of us could swim.

We panicked.

I told Bertie to get out to see how deep the water was. She slowly lowered one leg into the water, but when she got just above her knee she pulled her leg back in. It was early spring and the water was cold.

We were wearing our long-legged underwear with long black stockings pulled over it and high topped shoes, the uniform of the day for us until summer when we could go barefooted. I can see Bertie yet with one leg dripping wet, crying and saying she couldn't do it.

To make her see there was nothing to it, I stood up and jumped over the edge of the boat. I landed in water above my waist. As I'm writing this I'm wondering why I didn't take one of the oars and lower it into the water until it touched ground, pull it in and hold the wet end up by Bertie. That would have told us how deep the water was.

Bertie saw it wasn't so deep so she let herself down into the water. We waded to the closest shore, which was the one by the house. We left the boat with all our fishing gear and our little dog still in it.

We hurried to the house, dripping wet and very cold.

Dad asked us if Buster, the dog, was with us. We told him Buster was still in the boat and was afraid to jump out.

Dad said it would take all night for the boat to drift close enough to the

*Billie (in her brother's clothes) hitching Buster to the wagon to pull Bertie .*

south end of the lake so Miles could go down on his horse, ride out in the water and pull the boat ashore.

He asked if we had baited our fishhooks with the bacon yet. We said we had. Dad said that poor little Buster would probably get hungry before morning and try to eat the bacon and swallow the fishhook. Dad knew the dog wouldn't eat raw bacon. Feeling sorry for Buster all night was our punishment for disobeying.

Miles got Buster and the boat early the next morning. Buster was fine and very happy to be back with the family. Bertie and I put in a miserable night feeling sorry for our little Buster.

Here's a trick I pulled on Bertie that didn't turn out as planned. Bertie, as usual, owed me some favors. It was in the forenoon and it was hot. We were playing in the shade on the north side of the wash-house-meat house. I told Bertie as a favor she had to go make me a cold roast beef sandwich and bring it to me.

She did this and I ate it. I told her I wanted another sandwich.

I ate that one and told her I wanted another. (I was a big eater.) She went back in the house and brought me another sandwich. This one looked different than the other two, so I inspected it. I discovered that instead of butter, she'd used thin shavings of homemade soap.

I hadn't taken a bite of the soapwich, but I made Bertie think I had. I told her I would die unless she went into the meat house, climbed up on the rafters where Mama stored the duck and turkey feathers for future use and got me a long feather so I could tickle my throat and throw up. I lay down in the shade and began to moan and groan loud enough for her to hear me.

Bertie hurried in the little meat house and climbed up on the rafters. She was frantically trying to get a long feather when Dad walked in and asked what she was doing up there. She told him what had happened. She said she was trying to get a feather so Bill could make herself throw up.

Dad said, "AHH, soap won't kill her," and to get down from there before she fell. Bertie got down all right and went into the house. She left me lying on the ground, moaning and groaning. I didn't know what had happened until I finally got tired of being sick and went to see why Bertie didn't come back.

When I found her she told me what Dad had said. That was the end of Bertie doing whatever I told her.

Bertie told me just the other day that during our period of betting favors there were times she felt totally miserable. She just knew she would have to spend the rest of her life waiting on her big sister. That was when she got wise enough to tell Mama on me.

She also found out that crying helped make my scoldings or spankings bigger. From then on every time Bertie cried, I got paddled.

I realized Bertie was getting older and wiser (and even taller) than I. I had to find new ways to keep ahead of her and be the boss. Her getting taller than I was the hardest of all for me.

I tried every way I could think of to get taller. I hung from the rafters in the haymow until it felt my arms would come loose. Nothing helped. Poor little Bertie wound up being five feet four inches tall. The best I could do was five feet, one and three quarters inches.

Bertie also began to out-smart me regularly. This was when the "trying to outdo the other" started which lasted a few years. By the time we reached high school we were friends even though we had our stand-offs at times.

Now we are both shorter. I am four feet, eleven inches short and Bertie is five feet two inches tall. We are headed towards the sunset, arguing at times as we limp along. It does not matter who is the tallest, we are happy to still have each other.

## Chapter Six

# TRAPPING MUSKRATS

This story will be very hard to write. Times have changed and I have changed. Today I can't even kill a mouse.

Our ranch had a nice-sized lake in the south meadow. The lake was well populated with beautiful muskrats. During the winter when the fur was long and thick, their hides were worth good money. Fur coats for the rich people were all the go in those days. Every woman who had a fur coat was Somebody. Times have changed in that respect, THANK GOODNESS! But to make fur coats these beautiful animals had to be trapped, killed and skinned.

While writing stories for this book I feel like I'm dreaming backwards and this is the nightmare. I don't recall our exact ages when we started trapping. I'm guessing I was eight or nine. Bertie was, of course, two years younger, but she was always allowed to do new things as soon as I was.

At times I resented that. Since I was two years older I figured I should be able to do grownup things first. But I was glad to have her along while checking our traps at night just before our bedtime and again in the early morning about five o'clock. It was always spooky out after dark, especially so far from the house and carrying a kerosene lantern. Even our own shadows were scary, but we made ourselves do it. Checking our trap line at night was a time we needed each other.

The north end of our meadow lake started two city blocks south of our house and extended on south at least twenty more blocks. The muskrats lived in burrows or "muskrat runs" as we called them. They were dug back in the bank by the muskrats. The floor of the run was carpeted with moss. It was nice and round, just like the furry animal that made it.

The runs started at the edge of the lake, but underwater. The only way to find a run was to walk along the edge of the lake all bent over, tapping the ground with a hatchet. When we hit a tap that sounded hollow, we knew it was a run.

Using the sharp edge of the hatchet we cut a small square of ground. We kept the "lid" in one piece as a cover for the hole.

We lifted the top out and felt in the hole with one hand. If it was dry (no wet moss), it was an old run that had been abandoned. If it had a moss carpet, muskrats lived in it, so we set a trap and placed it in the hole.

The trap had a chain on it. A stake was driven through the chain. The stake held the trap and helped us find it when we came to check it.

The muskrats also built clever houses out in the middle of the lake. They used the moss that grew on the bottom of the lake. The houses were built each fall before the lakes froze over. Each house extended three feet above the water and was rounded on top, looking something like an Indian hogan or a haystack.

Inside the houses were tiers and ledges built as runways so the muskrats could easily climb to the top and be out of the water. This was where they lived out of the water. This was their home.

I wish I could interview a muskrat. There are so many things I would ask him, such as, "Is each and every rat an architect or are there just certain ones that know how to build those high tech houses?"

I used to think the higher-class animals lived in the houses and the poorer, unintelligent rats lived in the banks. It seemed the ones with the most luscious fur came out of the houses. I would like to ask a muskrat about that. I would like to ask him why he abandoned one run and built another.

Miles started trapping each fall as soon as the weather grew cold enough to make the animal's fur grow long and thick. This applied to the coyotes and skunks as well. Those animals were also killed (either shot, trapped or poisoned) for their fur.

For obvious reasons, skunks were not popular with trappers. (More later about my two skunks. My skunk career was just two skunks long, but still very clear in my head eighty years later.)

Miles trapped the muskrat runs in the banks until the lake froze over and he could get to the houses where trapping was better. Miles, of course, started trapping years before Bertie and I were big enough to handle it.

To set a trap we had to be heavy enough to step on the big iron spring with one foot and hold it down while opening the jaws of the trap with our hands. We then placed the little piece of iron hung there for that purpose over one jaw of the trap and secured it under the paddle in the center of the trap. As soon as we were able to do this safely we were ready to trap.

By the time Bertie and I started trapping, Miles had replaced his small two-jaw traps with bigger, four-jaw traps that killed the animal when it sprung. Now he did not find just a little chewed off foot in a trap if he was late checking his trap line.

Miles gave his two little sisters all of his old two-jaw traps. We had gone with him enough while he was trapping that we pretty much knew how to do it. But now we were on our own.

We could only trap on Saturdays and Sundays, as we had to go to school during the week. We either set our traps (which was the biggest job) on Friday night or Saturday morning. If we got them out on Friday evening we had to check them again before nine o'clock (bedtime). That was when we would light the kerosene lantern which didn't give much light but allowed us to locate the stakes and trap chains of the traps we had set out three or four hours earlier.

When we found one of our stakes, we lifted the lid off the hole. If there was a muskrat in the trap he would pop up out of the hole. That is when we hit and killed him with the blunt edge of the hatchet. If the chain was tight, we pulled until the trap came out with the rat in it so we could kill him.

We stepped on the big spring to open the jaws of the trap, took out the dead rat and reset the trap. Carrying that rat by the tail, we went on to our next trap. A few times we would find a sprung trap with a muskrat foot in it. The poor fellow chewed his leg off to make his getaway. There were some three-legged rats in our lake.

After checking our trap line (as we liked to call it) we carried our rats back to the house, left them on the porch and went to bed.

We had to do this all over again about five o'clock in the morning. We checked our traps twice during the daylight, which was child's play to us. Sunday evening as we made our nine o'clock run, we took our traps up. We had to go to school the next morning.

During Christmas vacation we had two weeks and trapped seven days a week. The muskrat had to be skinned without damaging the hide or fur. Miles, bless his heart, skinned all the rats we caught.

The hide was put on a stretcher with the fur inside and stretched as far as it would go. After the hide was dried or cured just right, the hides were bundled up and sent to a fur company. Miles shipped his sisters' hides separate from his. Soon we received a check for our furs.

Today I wish I could tell those rats how sorry I am that I did that.

## Chapter Seven

# SKUNK STORY

Trapping muskrats got to be old hat. I wanted to try something more grown up. Miles had caught several coyotes and a few skunks, but he wouldn't help me trap them. That made me all the more determined.

I found some old traps that weren't in use. I set one out in the hills about a mile from the house. My horse was used to having traps carried on her. I remember I had a trap, a stake and a hammer to drive the stake into the ground to secure the trap.

Day after day I rode out to look at my trap. I never did catch a coyote, I am now happy to say.

I thought I would try for some skunks. I trapped for these cute little black and white animals out around the ranch buildings. It was easy and right off I caught a skunk. He was dead when I found him in the trap. He barely smelled like a skunk. I took him out of the trap, reset it and carried my prize catch to the barn. I put him with the rats Miles had caught that morning. I thought he would surely skin my skunk as he had all my muskrats in the past.

Miles skinned his rats and left my skunk laying there. I had watched Miles skin many skunks and knew the skinner had to be very careful and not cut into that little sack under the tail. If that happened you might say the little skunk had the last word.

I waited until no one was around the barn and hung my skunk up by the back legs, got a sharp knife and skinned my skunk. I knew I had done a good job. I got the skin on a stretch board and hung up to dry.

I still had to get rid of the skunk carcass. Miles always threw the muskrats and coyote carcasses in the pigpen. So that's what I did with my skunk. It produced the worst skunk odor we ever had around the ranch.

Miles shipped my skunk hide off with his next shipment of furs. I got seventy-five cents for that beautiful fur. Sometime before that winter was over I went to Sutherland to visit a friend, Beulah Thomas.

Beulah was a city girl but she liked horses and had her own horse. We had gotten acquainted little by little over the years at rodeos or roundups as we called them in those days. I now had seventy-five cents and felt like going visiting. Beulah had asked me down to stay all night with her. I rode to Sutherland with Charley Coker, our mailman.

*Beulah Thomas on her horse at a roundup.*

The next morning we dressed and went downstairs. I had never seen a house where the heat came up out of the floor. We were standing over the furnace grate enjoying the heat drifting up. I was wearing a sweater with my seventy-five cents in the pocket. I stooped over to put my hand on the grate and dropped my skunk money down the furnace.

Skunk Number Two! After the first skunk experience I decided to bring in my skunk traps. I was through with skunks.

Before I got them all in, I caught another pretty black and white skunk. He, too, was dead when I found him. I brought him in to skin him.

I knew now to bury the carcass. I was an experienced skunk skinner. I hung him up, got my sharp knife and went to work.

I'd gotten the skin on the legs opened up and was working under the tail with too much confidence. I stuck the point of the knife into the "smell sack." Of course, I didn't want anyone to know what I'd done but there was no way to hide it.

I finished skinning the skunk and buried the carcass. That was the end of my skunk career.

*While this is not the greatest picture, you can see the cars lined up along the top of the hill to watch what was happening at a rodeo/roundup.*

*Some of the cowboys who participated in a rodeo/roundup.*

# Picking Up Cow Chips

On a ranch there are lots of kid jobs. I feel that we kids, all four of us, were somewhat useful and pretty much earned our board and room from ages five or six on.

I remember warning Mama that if she didn't treat me better I was going to go out and get myself a job working for my board and room and 'tobacca.' That's what the summer hired hands did during the winter in the sandhills. They found a ranch and worked for their keep and it always included their tobacco.

Neither keep nor tobacco cost much in those days. The meat was grown on the ranch. A sack of Bull Durham cost a nickel and the papers to roll the cigarettes came free with the shirt pocket-sized sack of Bull Durham. Everything else was homemade or homegrown. The bedrooms were the same temperature inside as the temperature outdoors.

Of all the jobs, the most hated one was picking up cow chips. The whole family hated it, but it had to be done once a year. Cow chips provided the fuel we used in the kitchen range.

We burned coal in the living room heater, but that cost money and had to be freighted by team and wagon from a town down on the railroad, usually Hershey. The trip to Hershey with a team and freight wagon took two days, so we went easy on the coal and burned cow chips in the kitchen range. But it took many wagonloads of chips to last a year.

The chips made a fast, hot fire. There was no temperature gauge on the oven, but Mama knew just how to feed that stove to get the right temperature for what she was cooking. It took lots of chips for a real hot fire for baking bread or biscuits.

If something was boiling too hard on top of the stove, Mama simply moved it to the back of the stove. It was less hot back there.

All the wonderful beefsteak that came off that stove was cooked in a big skillet on the front of the stove (the hot part). To make the gravy, the skillet was moved to a cooler place.

I remember that kitchen as very cozy. We did a lot of living in the kitchen on cold winter days. When Mama wasn't baking we left the oven door open. If someone came in with cold feet they pulled up a chair and sat in front of the oven door until they thawed out.

Back to picking up cow chips. Dad hitched a gentle team of old horses to the big lumber wagon. We needed gentle horses as they had to be trusted to stand and sleep while we all picked up a circle of chips around the wagon.

After Dad got the horses and wagon ready, the family climbed in. There was an old leaky washtub or a bushel basket for each chip picker but Bertie and me. We were too small to handle one alone so we shared a washtub.

We drove out to a pasture well studded with cow chips just right for gathering. Each person got out of the wagon, took a tub or basket and headed for what looked like a good chip picking spot. When the container was full, they took it back and emptied the chips into the wagon.

When Bertie and I took our tub, she always wanted to go one direction and I wanted to go another. We'd get that settled and get a few chips in our tub, but then Bertie would see a nice big chip that looked just right and I'd see one in the opposite direction that looked good to me. There were many standoffs. She would pull on her handle and I would pull on mine.

Mama or Dad often stepped in, hollered and told us which direction to go. Neither of us would argue with Mama or Dad.

When our tub was full we carried it to the wagon and waited for a bigger person to get there to empty it for us.

*Miles in front of the chip pile on Ol' Snip when she was young.*
*Behind his saddle is a coyote he trapped.*

After we cleared a large circle around the wagon, Dad picked up the reins, slapped the old horses on their rumps and drove to a new spot that looked good. We kept this up until the wagon was full.

Sounds boring. Well, it WAS and the wind was always blowing. At least the folks knew where we were and what we were or weren't doing.

The loads of chips were hauled to a place about sixty feet from the kitchen door and a chip pile was built. The chip pile resembled a big haystack when it was finished.

A wall was built of cow chips laid flat one on top of the other, just like the sod houses were built. As the wall grew, other chips were dumped inside. This was filled up and rounded off on top and covered with a layer of big flat chips, making it mostly waterproof. Now in rainy weather we could always get dry chips.

In front of the range in the kitchen was a large wooden box known as the Chip Box. Another kid job was to keep that Chip Box full of chips, at least never let it get empty.

It was fun to sit on the edge of that box and watch Mama cook. It was a good time to ask her questions or tell her something that was important to me, maybe a dream that puzzled me or how the new skimmer calf stuck his head right down in the bucket and went to drinking.

## Chapter Nine

# MILKING COWS

**O**ne of the biggest chores on the ranch was milking the cows. I didn't hate it as much as picking up cow chips each fall, but it was with us year around, twice a day.

My older brother Miles and my little sister Bertie and I usually did the milking. Miles milked the cows that had big teats or the ones that you had to squeeze hard to get the milk. Bertie and I milked the easier ones. Mama helped when she had time. Dad hated milking and only helped when necessary.

After each milking, the milk was run through the separator, separating the cream from the milk. The separator was anchored to the north porch floor right by the kitchen door. There was a four gallon heavy aluminum bowl on top of the separator frame. We poured the milk into a strainer that had several thicknesses of cloth. This took out all the barnyard dirt. It must have worked as that cloth would be plenty black at times and no one of us ever got sick from dirty milk or cream.

The separator was turned by hand and that was Miles's job. When he got the separator going at the right speed he would turn on the spout that let the milk out of the big bowl to start it through all the apparatus that took the cream out of the milk. The thick heavy cream came out one spout and the thin milk came out of the other spout.

From the morning milking we saved two one-gallon pails of milk for the family to drink that day, one gallon for dinner at noon and one for supper that night. The six of us drank two gallons of milk a day. Could this be the reason Bertie and I each are still chewing with the same teeth that God gave us to start with?

What was left of the milk was carried out and poured into the pig trough. The pigs thrived on it also.

From the cream spout we had all the thick yellow cream we needed for our cereal, puddings and fruit. What was left of the cream was poured into a five-gallon cream can. I don't remember how long it took to fill the cream can. It seemed forever.

When the cream can was full, Mama tied a tag on its handle and the next mail day Charlie, the mail carrier, hauled it to Sutherland where it was put on a train with many other five or ten gallon cans of cream and shipped to a creamery. About a week later Mama would receive a "cream check." The amount of the cream checks varied, but there was always one to ninety-nine cents on the end of the dollars.

One day Mama told Bertie and me that she was going to start dividing the cents on each cream check between us and that would be our allowance. As I dream back on this it was so much more fun than receiving a quarter or a dime once in a while. After a can of cream was shipped, the excitement was always with us until the check came back on the mail run. We could hardly wait for Mama to open the letter with the cream check in it. The fun was learning the amount of the cents (we weren't interested in the dollars) at the end of the dollars. Again I look back and see how Mama tried to make life interesting for those two little girls who nearly drove her crazy at times with their fussin'.

Mama liked to milk. It could be a very relaxing time. She sat there on her one-legged milk-stool holding a large milk pail between her knees. (When I first learned to milk, my pail was a one-gallon syrup bucket.) Her head nestled into the cow's flank. The cow stood very still, perhaps chewing her cud. She was contented and enjoyed giving her milk. The only noise was the milk squirting into the pail.

I suppose today the experts would say milking cows by hand was therapeutic. Maybe it was. There were no nervous breakdowns in our family during that time.

As I think back on it, Mama could be alone with her thoughts while she was milking, no kid asking questions or demanding her time in any way.

However, I do remember one time standing by Mama while she was milking. The cow was one of the newer ones and not as gentle as the older ones. I had heard of cows being touchy. I thought it meant you could touch them.

I asked Mama if the cow she was milking was touchy and she said, "Yes."

I reached over and touched it. The cow kicked Mama and ran to the opposite side of the corral. In the process she spilled Mama's almost full pail of milk. There was milk on Mama as well as on the ground.

I got a not-so-mild spanking right there on the spot, even though I told Mama I thought touchy meant I could touch the cow. I don't remember if Mama was able to finish milking that cow or not. My memory stops with the spanking. I still feel guilty for making that cow kick Mama.

During the warm weather, spring, summer and fall, we milked the cows out in the corral. Milking was done late in the evening and the whole world seemed to be quiet and peaceful at that time.

There was one thing I had to worry about and that was hearing coyotes howl out in the hills. One coyote would howl and receive an answer from another coyote on another hill. I liked hearing those coyotes if Miles was there in the corral with me. It frightened me and gave me the creeps if I was alone.

At times Miles would make the sound of a coyote just to tease me. One evening I was milking and heard what sounded like coyotes howling. I was sure Miles was still in the corral milking.

I said, "You're not foolin' me. I know that is you and not a coyote."

I finished my cow, got up and looked for Miles. He wasn't there but the coyotes were still howling. It was hard for a short kid with short legs to carry a bucket full of milk held out to the side so as not to hit the bucket with her leg as she ran. But I must have made it without spilling the milk, as I don't recall getting a spanking. I do remember the scolding I got for being afraid of coyotes that were a mile or more away.

Although milking a cow was a one-kid job, there was a problem that caused trouble between my sister and me. We each had our specific cows to milk if there was an even number of cows. If there was an extra cow and we were each just finishing the cow we were milking, we would both slow down, making our cow last as long as we could, hoping the other would get up and go to the other cow.

One Saturday morning neither of us would give in. Our cows were close enough together that I could hear Bertie wasn't getting any milk in her bucket. So I got up, put my milk stool away, took my bucket of milk and headed for the house. By the time I got to the house, there was Bertie right behind me, mad as heck.

We left the milk on the porch to be run through the separator. Bertie dashed into the kitchen ahead of me. Mama was at the stove getting breakfast. Bertie told Mama I wouldn't milk that last cow. I told Mama I thought Bertie should have to milk that cow.

Mama made me go back to the barn and milk that blasted cow. As I said before, sitting milking a cow is a great time for thinking, so I thought as I was milking that cow, "I'm tired of being treated this way and I'll just run away from home. After all I'm twelve years old and plenty able to take care of myself. I'll just get myself a job and it won't be milking cows, and today is a good day to do it. Besides after I'm gone, Bertie will have to milk my share of the cows."

## Chapter Ten

# I Run Away From Home

Sutherland was thirty miles south of the ranch. Our mail came up from Sutherland twice a week, Tuesdays and Saturdays. A young man by the name of Charlie Coker carried the mail for many years and we knew him very well.

Charlie carried the mail in an old nineteen-twenty Ford roadster. With the twisty, sandy roads, and twenty or more barbed wire gates to stop, open, drive through, get out, close, get back in the car and take off at a pace of ten miles an hour, it was about noon before the mail reached the ranch.

Saturday Mama had a lunch ready for Charlie as usual. While he ate, Mama sorted the mail and got it ready for the return trip to Sutherland. Mama would be busy and that was when I would make my getaway.

There was already a ladder up to the attic window. Someone had neglected to take it down the last time it was used. That was another piece of good luck for me.

On top of that, Mama had given me my allotment from the last cream check. I now had a dollar and thirty-five cents. I figured it was enough money to get me to Texas, as that was where I had decided to go. I knew my ride to Sutherland with Charlie wouldn't cost me anything.

When I reached Sutherland I planned to stay all night at a friend of Mama's and that wouldn't cost anything either. Mama, Bertie and I had stayed all night with Mrs. Hasket a few years back, so I felt it would be all right for me to go there.

The next morning I would somehow find the depot and see if one dollar and thirty-five cents would get me to Texas on the train.

I checked the ladder again and it was still there. The attic window was easy to crawl through. I watched from my bedroom window upstairs. The bedroom was right next to the attic. Finally I saw the mail car coming up the road from the south.

Charlie always parked in the same place, just in front of the barn, about one hundred feet from the kitchen door where Mama would be working.

I waited long enough for Charlie to get in the house and get settled. I took my suitcase, climbed through the attic window, slipped down the ladder and hurried up and got into the mailman's car. So far so good, but as I looked up straight in front of me, Dad was just about a mile away, coming out of the hills. I tried to hunker down out of sight.

I watched the house for Charlie to come out and watched Dad get closer and closer on that horse. Dad was riding a most beautiful horse named Antelope. I got a lump in my throat seeing Dad on Antelope. I loved to see Dad ride that horse. I still had to get out of there though, so Bertie would have to milk my share of the cows.

At last Charlie came out the kitchen door. It seemed to me he was just moseying along. When he finally reached the car, he was surprised to find me waiting for him. I told him I was just going down to Sutherland to visit Mrs. Hasket. He did ask some questions but he cranked up his car and we took off.

The road turned south a few feet from the barn. Dad was coming from the east and hadn't gotten close enough to see me in the car. I'd made my getaway. I was on my way to Texas and things were getting exciting.

I shortened Charlie's time getting back to Sutherland as I knew how to drive his Ford through the gates. He didn't have to get back in his car and drive through himself. He got out, opened the gate and pulled it back. I scooted over under the wheel and drove through. I scooted back to my side while Charlie closed the gate and got back in the car.

It was wintertime. The days were short and it was almost dark when we reached Sutherland. Everyone in Sutherland knew where everyone else lived, knew every dog and cat on sight, knew the name of each and who the animal belonged to. Charlie knew where Haskets lived. He dropped me off there.

Mrs. Hasket was a widow lady. Her sixteen-year-old daughter Letha lived with her. They were surprised to see me but they made me feel very welcome. I was enjoying it all and felt so grown up.

The next picture in my mind is when we were at the supper table. We were eating dessert, home canned peaches with thick heavy cream. (Here comes the good part, the part you've been waiting for.) Mrs. Hasket's big wall phone rang. It was the loudest I ever heard a phone ring and for some reason my stomach felt very squeegy.

Mrs. Hasket looked at me and said, "Your mama probably wants to know if you got here O.K."

She answered the phone. It was a short conversation.

She returned to the table, looked at me and smiled as she said, "Your mama and Miles are coming after you tonight."

Suddenly I felt like a kid who had done something terribly wrong.

I don't remember Mama and Miles arriving at Haskets to get me. It had to have been late as it would have taken four hours to make the trip.

The next thing I remember of that evening was laying down in the back seat of the old Ford on the way home and feeling very ashamed. Mama didn't talk to Miles. Miles didn't say anything to Mama. No one talked to me. I kept my mouth shut. This happened for the next four hours, all the way home.

Thinking back on it all, and knowing my mama as I did later on and the pride she had in her family, she must have been terribly ashamed and hurt by what her daughter had done.

All the way home I wondered what my punishment would be. My biggest fear was that the folks would not call me to help with the milking the next morning. I wanted things to go back to the way they were before I ran away.

It had to have been two o'clock by the time we got back. They did call me to go milk the next morning. My running away from home was never mentioned by Mama or Dad where I could hear it.

I found out later that Charlie had called from Sutherland to ask the folks if they knew I had ridden to Sutherland with him and had gone to Haskets.

Bertie told me the whole family was out looking for me in all the out buildings, behind all the haystacks in the meadow (between twenty or thirty), even in some blowouts out in the pastures a mile or so from the house. I had never thought of the family going to all that trouble for me. It kinda pleased me, which turned out to be all the pleasure I got out of running away from home.

Bertie also told me Mama was so sad she couldn't eat any supper. She only drank a glass of milk with tears running down her face. I think Bertie wanted to make me feel as bad as possible. Well, she did.

There was a thing between Bertie and me as to which one of us was the black sheep of the family, Bertie knew it was me and I wasn't so sure it wasn't. We had heard Mama say once that there was a black sheep in every family. She described to us what a black sheep was. Bertie thought the description fit me to a T and looked right at me. She said to Mama, "Bill is the black sheep of our family."

Mama chuckled embarrassed like and added, "Our family doesn't have a black sheep." I still felt it might be me.

After I ran away there was no question. IT WAS ME!

From then on for the next three years until Dad leased the ranch and the family went to the west coast for five years, I felt everyone I saw pointed at me and said, "There's Billie Snyder. Did you know she ran away from home?" I know it was discussed among the neighbors for we all minded each other's business. The way it was done was not bad-at least not all bad.

I do know that I was the only kid in the sandhills to have run away from home in the nineteen twenties and it didn't do my twelve-year-old reputation any good.

## Chapter Eleven

# SPENDING MONEY

Kids on a Sandhill ranch had no way to make spending money.

There were no paper routes, no daily papers, no lawns to mow. If the grass in the yard got too tall we just turned a gentle horse into the yard and he would enjoy shortening it.

There were no baby-sitting jobs as people always took all their kids with them when they went any place. Besides, if there was a "doings" going on, the potential baby sitters wanted to go, too. To this day a baby sitter would starve to death in the sandhills.

There was no big need to have money but it was nice to have some if we were lucky enough to be taken to North Platte. The folks only went to town when absolutely necessary. It could be many weeks between trips and they didn't often bother taking us along. We got to go only two or three times a year. We sure needed money then so we could go to the Dime Store.

We bought things such as jackknives and lipstick, anything that wasn't more than a dime. I don't remember ever buying candy. We knew Dad would buy us a small sack of hard candy when he bought the groceries.

One time on the ride to North Platte Bertie and I decided we were big enough to have beautiful white skin like our schoolteachers and the girls in town. We made a raid on the Dime Store. We bought greasy vanishing cream (it was the cheapest), very white face powder and real red lipstick. We could hardly wait to get home and apply our makeup.

Miles had the milk cows in the corral and ready to milk when we got home. Bertie and I had to change our clothes, grab our milk buckets and hike out to the corral to help with the milking.

When milking was over, supper was ready.

By the time supper was over and the dishes done, it was too dark for us to see to put on our makeup.

The next morning we hurried through our chores. We ate our beefsteak, biscuits and gravy fast. We zipped through clearing the table, washing the breakfast dishes (including the milk separator), and ran upstairs to put our makeup on.

We wound up looking like a couple of ghosts with very red lips. We soon forgot about trying to look like the girls in town and kept on being a couple of country ranch kids.

# GOING TO SCHOOL

I started to school in September, nineteen-eighteen. I had turned six in April. Miles was twelve and in the seventh grade.

The schoolhouse was a little one-room frame building with two narrow windows on the west and two on the east. The school sat out in the Sandhills, five miles from our house, no other buildings in sight, only a windmill about an eighth of a mile away. The bigger kids carried buckets of drinking water from the windmill when it ran, but mostly it didn't, so each family brought one or more bottles of water from home.

The one door to the building was on the south. That was where we came in and went out unless someone decided to climb through a window. I remember doing that a few times. I even remember one of our teachers crawling out a window. It was fun.

The north end of the schoolhouse was a solid wall with a large blackboard in the center. Above the blackboard was the picture of the current United States president. The day I started school the first thing I learned was that Woodrow Wilson was the President of the United States.

The teacher's desk was placed in front of the blackboard facing the south. There were two rows of desks facing north, one row on the west wall and the other along the east wall. The front seat in each row was the smallest, for kids five or six years old. Each seat going back was bigger than the one in front. The last seats were for the seventh and eighth graders.

The desk seats were all double. There were five seats in each row. Bertie says that when she started to school her feet didn't reach the floor when sitting at her desk in the front row.

The teacher's chair was a captain's chair and the only chair in the building. Usually when a parent visited school, they sat at one of the eighth grader's desks.

One day Mama visited school. No one knew she was coming until she showed up. We, the teacher and the kids, got very nervous, each one trying to do their best.

Mama was dressed in her good riding habit, but for some reason she was riding a lazy, slow horse named Chief. No one ever rode Chief if there was another horse available, so along with Mama's good riding habit she was wearing one spur. She always wore that spur when she had to ride Chief.

There was a spacious fenced-in yard around the schoolhouse. When Mama arrived and came through the gate into the schoolyard. She tied Chief's bridle reins to a fence post and came on in the schoolhouse.

Our teacher was a woman we all liked very much. Her name was Mabel Guston. She pulled her chair out from her desk and over to the side by a window. Miss Guston had Mama sit in her chair and she (Miss Guston) stood behind her desk while teaching.

Mama happened to look out the window and saw Ol' Chief trying to rub his bridle off against the fence post. Mama stood up fast and started for the door to get to Chief before he got his bridle off. Chief was lazy but also a little ornery and she knew he would be hard to catch to rebridle.

In her hurry Mama caught her spur on the front rung of the teacher's big chair and dragged it a few steps behind her. We all laughed, including Mama. (Mama loved slapstick). Anyway everyone relaxed and Mama reached Ol' Chief in time.

There were several pastures between our place and school, which meant several barbed-wire gates. Miles was still in school so he opened all the gates. All I had to do was ride.

Miles had outgrown the kid's saddle years ago and it was mine now. The stirrups had been shortened to my size, which was as short as they could be buckled up. I rode that saddle to school several years. As I grew the buckle was let down another inch.

After I'd gone to school for a few days, Miss Guston asked the folks if there was some way they could get four-year-old Bertie to school. She said she would like to see what she could teach Bertie.

The folks said, "No problem."

But there was a problem. There was only one saddle left and that was Dad's big saddle. On days Bertie went to school, Dad would be without a saddle. Still they put Dad's saddle on the only really gentle horse on the ranch and lifted Bertie into it.

The reins were knotted together and looped over the saddle horn. All Bertie had to do was hang on to the saddle with both hands and old Roany would take her those five miles to school. He just followed along with Miles and me and our horses.

Bertie's first day at school is so vivid in my mind. Bertie was a nervous little kid and had a problem of wetting her pants when she was very nervous. The teachers always gave their attention to the youngest pupils first. I don't remember anything being done to make Bertie feel at home.

As soon as school opened the teacher put her chair up to the blackboard and Bertie climbed up and stood facing that scary blackboard with a piece of chalk in her hand. Miss Guston wanted to see if Bertie knew her ABCs. Bertie just stood there. She didn't cry, but the water began to run down her legs. The depression in the seat of the chair filled up.

When Bertie was finished peeing, she climbed out of her chair with her back still to the audience, took a handkerchief out of her little apron pocket and tried to mop it all up. I don't remember what was done to clean Bertie up. I just remember the embarrassment of seeing her pee her pants in front of the whole school.

I don't know how many days Bertie went to school riding Dad's big saddle, hanging on to the saddle horn. It was long enough for Bertie's baby bottom to become red and raw from rubbing against that saddle seat. She had no way to lift herself up off the saddle for even a second.

I ran across my old report for the winters of nineteen-eighteen and nineteen-nineteen. I attended school thirty days that year. It shows I completed the first grade and went into the second grade in the fall.

Bertie had no report card. The next fall she started in the first grade. By then Dad had bought another kid's saddle.

Our report cards for that year show us attending school for sixty days. Bertie passed from the first grade to the second and I passed from second to third. Our teachers were often just out of high school with a few weeks in teacher's training. It was up to our teacher whether she passed us or not.

There was only one kid in our school who did not pass to the next grade each year. His name was Dutch. More about Dutch later.

*Miles flew his kids to school. This is Miles and*
*his oldest son Jim next to Miles' plane .*

## Chapter Thirteen

# TRAVELING TO SCHOOL

As I remember, we allowed an hour for the trip to school. Bertie and I got to sleep until it was time to get dressed and ready for school.

There were mornings when Bertie and I had to roll out at four or five o'clock. Those were the times Dad found a baby calf that was about not to make it. When that happened Dad carried the calf into the kitchen and placed him on the floor in front of the open oven door. We would hear Mama call, "Kiddies, get down here and rub this baby calf warm."

I always felt that when Mama called us "kiddies" in the mornings she was sorry she had to make us get up so early.

There would be two gunnysacks on the tiny calf. Bertie and I knew what to do. We each took a gunnysack in our hands and vigorously rubbed the weak baby calf. We kept it up until the calf could bawl pretty loud and get up on his wobbly legs. Then he was ready to go back out in the cold to his mama.

We liked that job. The baby calves were so cute.

Miles helped Dad with the morning chores. Mama cooked a big breakfast. There were a lot of pancakes and oatmeal with real cream, just the way it came out of the separator.

A breakfast I can still taste today was beefsteak, biscuits and thick gravy made with milk in the frying pan that the steak was fried in. Mama put up three dinners while getting breakfast.

Dad smoked a pipe and smoked Union Leader tobacco. The tobacco came in pretty, red tin boxes with handles. The boxes were just the right size for a one-kid dinner box. We each had a sack in which we put our Union Leader dinner box along with a bottle of water and anything else we were taking to school that day.

Each kid's sack was tied on her saddle with the leather strings that were put there as decoration. Dad seemed to think we wouldn't amount to anything if we didn't eat lots of beef, not just meat, it had to be beef.

On days that we had beefsteak, biscuits and gravy for breakfast, Mama fried an extra steak for each kid's dinner at school. This went in the dinner bucket last, on top of the sandwiches, which were made of jelly.

Dad made several two-day trips to town each fall and brought home apples, pears and peaches, along with other winter supplies. Mama made lots of jellies and jams from the fruit. She also made oodles of strawberry and tomato butter from her own garden.

Fruit had to be gotten when it was in season. One year Dad didn't get any fruit hauled out. That winter all we had for sandwiches was the strawberry jelly and the tomato butter plus the beefsteak. To this day I can't eat strawberry jelly or tomato butter.

If we trotted or loped our horses riding to school, our dinners were jumbled

*A friend, Mae Stelzer, on her horse, Billie on gentle Snip, and Bertie on old Roany.*

when we opened them at the first recess. (We always had a snack out of our dinner at first recess.) If we didn't clean up our dinner at noon, we finished it at last recess or after school let out at four o'clock before we got on our horses and headed home.

Unless there was a reason to hurry home or get to school, we just let our horses mosey along. We didn't know it then but we were enjoying nature.

My most vivid memory of this is riding at a slow walk on warm sunny mornings, looking at the ground and counting the cobweb doilies we saw in the grass. The doilies were covered with the morning dew. If we caught them just right, with the sun shining on the dew, it looked like a circle of thousands of diamonds.

We rode faster when it was cold or we had a reason to hurry. When school let out on Tuesdays, we grabbed our sacks, tied them on our saddles and we were on our way home. Tuesday was the day the mail came up from Sutherland.

The folks took the Omaha World Herald. It was a daily paper so we received three papers on Tuesdays. The main one was the Sunday paper. It had all the funnies. It was something to look forward to. On Saturday we received the other four papers for the week.

We were the only family in school to have a phone. You could only have a phone if the phone wire went by your house. We were the lucky ones. If Mama heard of a piece of earth shattering news, we would be in a hurry to get to school to tell it to the other kids.

Our school was only for seven months. All other schools in the Sandhills were either eight or nine months. I thought we were so lucky to only have to go to school seven months and all the other kids had to go longer. Besides it was fun to have our last-day-of-school picnic on April Fools Day, which happened a few times.

Our school year started on Labor Day, the first Monday of September, and was out the first of April, which left us going to school during the coldest part of the year. We missed many days of school each year due to cold weather and snow.

If we were sick we missed. All we ever had was a few colds each winter. We never had any childhood diseases while going to school in the Sandhills. The bugs for those illnesses must have either died of old age or froze to death before reaching the kids in the hills.

We had all those diseases much later in life when we didn't have Mama to care for us. I had scarlet fever in 1937 when I was twenty-five-years old. I had to hire a nurse to come and care for me. Scarlet fever patients were quarantined for three weeks at that time.

I was thirty-six-years old when I had the whooping cough.

The most any of my report cards show me being in school for one year is six months. That was the year I did the eighth grade. We went to a different school that year and that was an eight-month school.

The year Bertie finished the second grade and I finished the third grade, Miles graduated from the eighth grade. That meant Miles wouldn't be going back to school the next fall. Bertie and I would ride to school alone. There were four barbed-wire gates between our house and the schoolhouse.

As time drew near for us to start back to school, Dad worked the gates over and made them easy to open. To open a barbed-wire gate takes strength and I barely had enough of that. I was short and couldn't put the push up where it should be.

The post at the end of the fence was solid in the ground. This post had two wire loops on it, one at the bottom. You put the bottom of the gate post in this loop. There was another wire loop at the top of the fence post. You put your shoulder against the gatepost and braced your feet and pushed with all your might until you got that top loop over the top of the gatepost. The gates were harder to close than they were to open.

Since Dad made all the gates on the way to school easy to open I could do it. There were times when Bertie and I went in another direction, maybe to visit some neighbor kids. We ran into some gates that were a two-kid job and Bertie got off and helped me.

## Chapter Fourteen

# Trouble With The Teacher

There were four families going to our school (District 58). There were three Clifford kids and three Pinkerton kids and two Snyder kids. There were two other boys, the Kirts boys, Jim and Dutch.

Jim and Dutch lived with their dad and their uncle in an old sod house about halfway between our place and school. The kids' mama had died a few years back. As they say, it was one of those sad situations.

The Kirts boys didn't go to school every year, but when they did, they joined Bertie and me as we rode by their place. Poor little Dutch never could get past the second grade and the teacher always kept him in at recess because he didn't have his lesson.

*The boys in school in front of the school house. Front row L to R: James Pinkerton, Jim Kirts, Dutch Kirts, and Harold Pinkerton. In Back is Clarence Pinkerton.*

The teacher either boarded at the Cliffords who lived only two miles from school or at our house. I don't know what determined where she stayed, but some years we had the teacher and some years Cliffords had her.

One year the teacher was staying at our house. This meant she rode horseback to school with Bertie and me. My horse was a gentle horse and I loved her. The teacher, I'll call her Vi, was given my beloved Midget to ride to school.

Vi jerked Midget's mouth with the bridle and mistreated her in other ways. It didn't take long for me to take an intense dislike to Vi.

Mama couldn't stand seeing Vi lick her knife at the table. Mama soon gave Vi her own private butter dish. It got to the place where we wouldn't keep her any longer. I guess Cliffords didn't think it could be all that bad so they took her in.

Vi was not a good teacher and she didn't get along with the kids.

After Vi moved to Cliffords, Bertie and I rode to school with Jim and Dutch. I'd been thinking I had a score to settle with Vi over the way she had treated my horse.

One morning I said to Dutch, "You always have to stay in so today, just before last recess, I'm going to do something so Vi will make me stay in, too. After the other kids are out in the yard, I'll make a dive for her. I'm going to make her sorry for jerking Midget's mouth. If I need help, I'll call you. Will you come up and help me?"

Dutch said he would.

Just before last recess I got out of my seat and walked to the door as if I was going to the privy without permission. Vi told me to sit down in my seat and to stay in all through recess. Things were working out as planned.

The other kids were let out for recess. As soon as the door closed, I made a dash for Vi. She grabbed me by the hair and I grabbed her by the hair. We were both bent over holding each other's head down.

I called, "Dutch, come and help me."

Vi said, "Floyd," (that was his real name) "stay where you are."

Dutch answered in a very weak voice, "I am."

So I yelled real loud for Bertie. She must have been standing right by the door listening. The door swung open and Bertie ran in and said, "Vi, you let go of Bill."

Then Bertie picked up a monkey wrench that we used as a hammer to drive nails in the wall. Bertie hit Vi on the head with the wrench.

Vi let go of my hair. I let go of hers. Bertie and I ran out of the schoolhouse.

The teacher called in the rest of the kids and locked the door with Bertie and me out. We kept hollering for her to let us get our coats so we could go home. She put up with that for a while, then opened a window and threw our wraps and saddle sacks out on the ground. Bertie and I got on our horses and rode home.

Bertie and I just renewed our memories of this. She says I told her to use the wrench. I say she saw the wrench on the desk and picked it up and used it on her own. We each feel we are right.

Bertie and I didn't go back to school. In a very short time there was a school board meeting at the schoolhouse with the three board members (Dad, Mr. Clifford and Mr. Pinkerton), the  county superintendent and the teacher present. Bertie and I were to be there also, in case they needed us for questioning.

I don't recall being called into the schoolhouse. I can still see myself with my ear glued to the door trying to listen to what was going on inside.

After investigating Vi's past record, they found she had been fired from her first school the year before because she couldn't get along with the older students. The superintendent said he had a school in the county with five younger students who needed a teacher. He thought that he could get her hired for that school if she would agree to quit teaching at our school.

That was agreeable with Vi, but it took some time. Our school went on as usual until they got the other school for Vi and hired a new teacher to finish out the year at District 58.

There was another schoolhouse five miles to the west of our house. We knew all the kids in that school and they had a good teacher. It was her second year at that school.

Dad made arrangements for us to transfer and finish the year over there. That was great, a different teacher, different friends and a different schoolyard for playing.

More kids rode horseback to school there. The yard was full of gentle old horses just standing with their bridle reins dragging, waiting for the seven hours to pass so they could go home and get turned out for the night.

There was a blowout in the schoolyard and that was where we played. We played rodeo, calling the blowout the corral. The big kids were the broncs and would get down on hands and knees. The little kids would get on their backs and get bucked off. The teacher rang the school bell at the end of recess. We kids raced for our seats leaving a trail of sand shaking out of our clothes. When I think of that school, I always see that blowout and all the fun we had in it.

My reputation was questionable after the trouble at our school and I felt it. The rest of the year at the new school I saw to being a model student as well as a good kid and won the prize for having the best deportment of the year.

*Bertie and Billie in a large blowout*

The next fall we went back to our old school and it did feel more like home. We were back with the Clifford and Pinkerton kids. There was no blowout in this schoolyard. There was a blowout just a few hundred feet outside the school yards fence, but we had to get permission from the teacher to go over there, so we played mostly in the school yard at recesses and noon.

We played kid games, Pump-pump-pull-away, Drop the Handkerchief and other games where we chased each other. When we couldn't get interested in a game we communicated among ourselves and sometimes ended up in a fuss.

The Cliffords drove a buggy to school. A gentle old mare named Roxy always pulled it.

One year Roxy had a cute little colt and, of course, the colt had to come to school so it could get its dinner from its mother. It just followed the buggy to school.

One day one of the Clifford kids and I were fussin'. To get the best of the fuss I said I was going to milk Roxy out on the ground so the colt would starve.

I got under Roxy and milked a few streams of her milk on the ground just to make it look like I meant it. I'd been wondering how easy it was to milk a horse and that was my chance. I would not have starved the colt for I thought it was cute and I loved to pet and play with it.

These were only a few things we did to amuse ourselves during our two fifteen-minute recesses plus what was left of our noon hour after we ate lunch. Neither of the schools we attended furnished a thing for the kids to play with or play on. One day when Bertie had Dad's saddle on her horse we got the bright idea of taking his coiled up throw rope off of it. We had a wonderful day jumping rope, but Dad could tell we'd tampered with it. He told us he knew what we'd done and not to do it again. We didn't.

There is something to be said for those poor kids who were our teachers up in the Sandhills in the early part of the twentieth century. They were just out of high school. They had graduated the previous May and had three or four weeks normal training during the summer to obtain a teacher's certificate.

It was hard to get eighteen-year-old girls to come up in the Sandhills, so far from civilization, to teach school. Our best hope was one who had romantic ideas of meeting and marrying a cowboy. There were always a few cowboys waiting to see what the new crop of schoolteachers was like. It was not unusual for a young horseman to find a reason to stop at an isolated schoolhouse to ask an urgent question, and always just after school had opened in the fall.

## Chapter Fifteen

# KIDS AT PLAY

**O**ne time we were visiting neighbors. There were several more kids there. We had gotten hold of a long rope. We stretched the rope out and tied the ends to secure objects leaving enough slack so a kid could sit on it with his feet touching the ground.

We kids took turns sitting on the rope, holding tight with both hands. One kid stood on each side of the kid on the rope, ready to jerk the rope up quick and high enough so the kid would swing back and be left hanging with his head down. Then he would be lowered to the ground and the next kid would get on. This was fun for a while but it soon got boring.

We decided to see how close we could get the kid's head to the ground but not actually hit it. That was more exciting.

*Left to Right: Bill, Bertie and Buster. I'm glad I wasn't a kids' Shetland pony.*

Bertie's turn came. She was the smallest kid playing. She sat on the rope and held on tight. In trying to get her head close to the ground, we got it too close and whacked her head on the hard ground. She crumpled in a heap.

The other kids were concerned and thought we should go in the house and get Mama. I told them that Bertie wasn't hurt but trying to make us think she was, so we dragged her up out of our way and went on playing.

I remember looking at her a time or two and thinking she was carrying this one on a bit too long. After a time she sat up looked around and asked where Mama was. We stopped playing then and took Bertie in the house where Mama and the other women were visiting.

Bertie's angel was sure on the job that day. Bertie says the first thing she remembers is sitting with her feet in a pan of water and all the women standing around looking at her.

It must not have hurt her as she is eighty-eight years old and, as near as I can tell, she is O.K. in the head.

*Billie pretending she is a trapper with her pelts and rifle. Buster is hitched to the wagon and stands in front of the chip pile with the barn in the background.*

## Chapter Sixteen

# An Ordinary Winter Evening On The Ranch

It is now December 2001. The evenings are turning cool and I am reminded of the evenings we spent on the ranch. I will try to describe them.

There was no computer, no television, not even a radio. We did have a big old-fashioned telephone on the west wall at the foot of the open stairway going up to the kids' bedrooms. (The telephone line came to our ranch sometime during 1917.) The phone very seldom rang at night. I guess the other ranchers were doing about the same as we were.

The only noises we heard that we didn't make ourselves were coyotes calling and answering each other out in the hills. On cold, clear nights we could hear their howls very plainly.

We had a pot-bellied heater set out a ways from the wall in the living room. Dad's big rocker and Mama's smaller rocker sat close to the heater.

After supper was over, Dad went in the living room, lit another lamp, picked up his current western magazine and started reading. Miles usually had a project going. His spot in the living room was at a long table we called the library table. That table was Miles's workbench.

One of Miles's projects was putting together a crystal set radio. It was something he ordered by mail. I'll never forget the excitement we all felt when at last he could get static on his radio.

There was one set of headphones but we divided the earpieces and two people listened in at once. Miles would give one headphone to one of us kids then he would tune around until we finally heard a voice off in the distance and we would holler with excitement.

One winter night a neighbor girl, Mae Stelzer, was spending the night with Bertie and me. Mae was eager to listen to Miles's radio. Miles gave her the whole head set. He adjusted it to her ears.

Soon her eyes lit up. She smiled big and said, "Oh, I hear a coyote."

As soon as supper was done, Mama's day's work was mostly over. She went to her

*Mae Stelzer, her sister Ruth and their Shetland pony colt at the Tregos.*

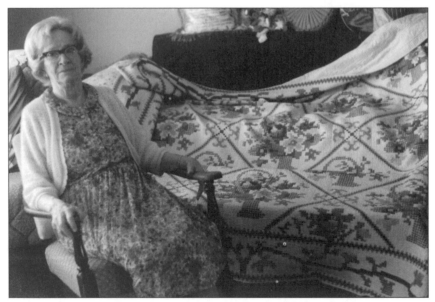

*Mama and one of her prize winning quilts. Over 85,000 patches are contained in this quilt.*

*The ranch house in the winter. Notice the chip pile on the right and the barn in the background.*

rocker in the living room. She either crocheted or cut and sewed quilt pieces.

After Bertie and I finished washing and drying the dishes, we went into the living room. The lamp from the kitchen was brought in. Now we had two lamps in the living room.

One night no one brought the kitchen lamp into the living room. It was sitting on the kitchen table. Dad went out in the kitchen to get it. As he picked the lamp up off the table, the bottom of the lamp caught on the back of a straight-backed chair that was pushed up to the table. That knocked the lamp out of Dad's hand.

We heard a loud noise and heard Dad say a bad word, which he usually didn't say around the house. We all hurried out in the kitchen to see what had happened. Dad had broken the lamp.

I think the same thought crossed Bertie's and my minds at the same time. Who is going to spank Dad? If Bertie or I broke anything, we got a spanking.

The flame in the lamp died before it hit the floor so all Dad had to do was clean up the coal oil and broken glass. It pleased Bertie and me to know that Dad could break something, too.

On some of the coldest nights Mama would make soup and a pie. We took our supper in the living room and ate huddled around the heating stove. That was always fun. It was like a picnic on the floor of the living room. Mama had the kettle of soup and the pie on the floor by her rocking chair and dished up the soup and passed it around.

One night I remember so clearly. It was potato soup and pumpkin pie we were having. Somehow I got in there too close and stepped in the soup. I was in a hurry to get out of the soup and stepped in the pumpkin pie. I don't know how old I was at the time but my foot was small enough, even with my big heavy shoe on it, to go in that soup kettle.

The whole family laughed at me, especially Dad. I couldn't stand to have Dad laugh at me. It sure hurts to be laughed at when you are a kid. There should be a law against laughing at a little kid when she makes a mistake.

Our living room was 16 by 16 feet square with a three-foot wide-open stairway taking up the north half of the west wall. There was a landing halfway up the stairs where the stairs made a square turn. There was a very nice banister going down the first half of the stairway. It was a favorite spot for Bertie and me. As Bertie says, it was the one spot in the house that we never had to dust. We loved sliding down that banister. Bertie did fall off once and was knocked out for a time. It seems she was always getting knocked out. She just now told me she saw a lot of stars when she was a kid.

Back to an evening by the fire. Miles was over in his corner, Dad was reading and Mama was crocheting.

If Bertie and I couldn't find any thing to do, Mama put her crocheting aside and played rummy with us. We had a backgammon board for a card table. Mama turned her rocking chair out into the room and Bertie and I each pulled up a chair and balanced the board on our laps. We played rummy, which was Mama's favorite card game.

Dad did not play rummy, but one night he laid his magazine down, pulled his chair up and put one side of the board on his lap. He took the cards and said he was going to teach us to play pitch. We learned enough that night for it to be fun.

I was anxious to get in the living room the next night to play more cards. As soon as we were all settled I said, "Dad, can we play some more of that buck?" Dad laughed at me again, but I could tell he wasn't punishing me with his laugh.

From then on when Bertie and I wanted to play cards at night, Mama and Dad put aside what they were doing and we played pitch until nine o'clock. That was bedtime for kids. Then Dad picked up his western magazine or a Zane Grey book and continued reading. Mama picked up her fancywork, be it crocheting or quilting.

Bertie and I went up to bed, hoping our bedroom had warmed up a little.

Here was a two-story frame house with no insulation. The only method of heating the upstairs was from the heater in the living room. There was no vent or heat register going from the living room into the upstairs rooms. Sometime during the evening one of us ran upstairs and opened the doors to the two bedrooms. Miles's bedroom was on the north of the hall and the girls bedroom was on the south.

Our bedroom grew very cold by morning. I always had to have a drink of water during the night. I'd take a tin cup of water with me and set it on the windowsill by the bed. Many mornings water was frozen to the bottom of the cup.

The little door into the attic also opened off the hall. The attic was a very interesting place. That was where we put the things we didn't use any more. It was fun to go up there and run on to things we had forgotten about. They seemed new again.

At the far end of the attic was a small window on hinges. That was my escape route the time I ran away from home

This brings to mind the folks' clothes closet. It was the space left under the stairway. The upper part of the stairs left enough room to hang a few clothes. People didn't have many clothes in the good ol' days and needed very little closet space.

There was an interesting shelf in that closet. It was where Mama hid things from us kids.

Under the lower part of the stairway was a big wooden box called the rag box. Everything that was good enough to make a rag was put in there.

By the time our living room carpet grew worn and thin, that rag box would be full and it was time for Mama, Bertie and me to start making carpet rags. Mama would bring out an armful of rags and a pair of scissors. She'd select a rag and start at one end and make a nitch with the scissors. She made niches an inch apart, depending on how thick the material in the rag was. Then it was up to Bertie and me to tear off the strips.

Soon the strips we tore off made a big pile. Then Mama got out her Brunswick (Monkey Wards) foot-pedal-driven sewing machine and sewed the ends of the strips together.

Bertie and I took turns sitting behind the sewing machine rolling the long string of rag that came out of the sewing machine into a ball. When the ball got too big to handle, we started a new ball.

Mama seemed to know when we had enough rag balls to make a carpet the size of the one that was worn out. She packaged the balls up and sent them to a place that did weaving. After many weeks we had a carpet just like the old one, only it was new and made us all feel good when we looked at it. I don't know what was done with the old rug, but I'll bet it was put to good use.

## Chapter Seventeen

# BORROWED PETS

Dad was good about getting us any animal we wanted. That is, if he could borrow it.

One day Bertie and I asked Dad if he would get us a Shetland pony. He asked us, "What in the world do you want of a Shetland when you have plenty of good horses to ride?"

We wanted a cute little Shetland to play with. Nothing more was said. It wasn't long before Dad came riding home one day leading a fat, short-legged, spotted Shetland pony.

Bertie and I, as usual, had climbed to the peak of the barn watching for Dad to come riding in out of the hills. He was late and we had been watching for some time.

We finally spotted him way up in the valley riding very slowly. There was a very short something coming along beside him. As he got closer we could see he had our Shetland pony. We were so excited we had a hard time waiting for him to get close enough for us to run out and meet them.

The first thing we asked was, "What's his name?"

Dad answered, "His name is Buster and his legs are so darned short it took all afternoon to bring him home."

The next question was, "Is he ours?"

*Billie on Buster. She is only pretending to be unhappy.*

"No," Dad said. "I just borrowed him for a while from a neighbor up north."

We couldn't wait to ride him. Right away Dad took the halter off that he had used to lead Buster home. He put a bridle on him and buckled it to fit.

A little kid does not mount a saddle horse. She climbs up the best way she can. She grabs the first highest thing she can reach on the saddle and pulls and squirms her way up to where she can get a foot in the stirrup and grab the saddle horn. Buster was so short it was no trouble for us to get on him bareback..

Bertie scrambled on our pony, took the reins in her right hand and Buster took off for the closest barbed wire fence. He scraped Bertie off as he easily ran under the fence. He did the same thing with me. We soon learned all of his tricks and he learned all of ours. The pony came out far ahead of us in tricks.

We found that we could handle Buster if he had a saddle on, but Buster was round and fat and he knew the horse trick of expanding his body as he was being cinched up. As we tried to tighten the cinch, he blew himself up. We weren't strong enough to tighten it then.

When we tried to get on, the saddle would turn. We would have to uncinch, take the saddle off and start all over again with the same results.

Buster must have loved this as all he had to do  was stand there. It turned out Dad had to saddle Buster for us or at least tighten the cinch. Dad didn't hesitate to let Bertie and me know that the little ol' pony was far smarter then we were.

I have one picture of Dad in my mind that I like to look at now and then. Dad was saddling Buster for me. He had thrown the blanket and the saddle on Buster and then just stood there with a smile on his face. He needed to check the cinch on the other side of Buster. He finally said, "Don't know whether to step over or go around." Then I knew Dad liked our cute little pony.

I finally tired of Buster and wanted a goat. I asked Dad if he thought he could borrow me a goat.

It wasn't long until Dad made a trip to Stapleton in the car. That evening when he drove in, he had a bright-eyed billy goat in the back of the car. To me this was even more exciting then when he came in leading Buster.

I fell in love with that goat. Naturally his name was Billy since he was a billy goat and he smelled like one. I didn't mind the smell at all. Other people noticed it at times.

Bertie was leery of Billy right from the start, but she would go along with the things I wanted to do with him. I had heard that goats would walk corral fences and eat tin cans. Those were the first things we tried.

We couldn't get him to take a tin can in his mouth. We worked a long time at

*Bertie, Towser, Buster and Billie*

trying to get him interested in the corral fence. We would lead him up to the fence and with one of us holding his halter rope in our hand, we would both climb up and sit on the top board of the eight-foot corral fence. We'd sit there and look down at Billy and try to talk him into coming on up. All the time he was looking up at us as if to say, "What are you kids doing up there?"

We finally decided our goat wouldn't walk a corral fence.

One day Dad was working in the barn. Bertie and I were leading Billy around looking for something to do. We got the bright idea of trying to get Billy up in the haymow.

We asked Dad if that would be all right.

He said, "Go ahead."

I got in front holding Billy's halter rope. Bertie got behind to push if necessary. Billy went up the stairs just fine. I think Dad was a little surprised that we got that goat up there.

So far so good. Then we grew tired of playing with the goat and decided to bring him down and put him back on his stake with the long rope so he could eat grass.

We led Billy to the stairs but he would not go down. We tried everything we could think of, but that goat would not start down the stairs.

We finally asked Dad what we should do. He said, "You got him up there, you get him down."

It never occurred to us to just go away and leave the goat up there.

Bertie and I held a conference and decided to fork a pile of hay out the haymow door on to the ground below. Our idea was to get a big enough pile of hay on the ground that we could push Billy out. He would land in the hay and not be hurt.

It worked. In fact, Billy jumped right into the hay. He was not hurt.

We didn't hear another word out of Dad. I think he just wanted to see what we would come up with. Dad was like that.

Billy wasn't all play. He also meant work for Bertie and me.

Billy was tied to a sharp-pointed stake with a fifty-foot rope. We drove that stake in the ground where the grazing was good. Thus Billy had a hundred-foot circle to graze.

When the grass got too short for grazing it was up to Bertie or me to move him to a new spot. We had to get our hammer, go pull up Billy's stake, lead him to better grazing and drive the stake in the ground with the hammer and be sure to get it in deep enough that Billy couldn't pull it out.

One summer forenoon I was in the house. Billy was staked on a little knoll west of the house just outside the barbed wire yard fence. Dad had planted trees outside the yard fence. There was another wire fence to protect the trees. That made two wire fences between Billy and the house. It didn't take long for Billy to eat all the grass he could reach from that stake. Someone had to move his stake to fresh, long grass.

Mama looked out the west window and said, "Billie, the goat's stake needs to be moved."

I started out the kitchen door and saw Bertie up by the barn. I called her and told her it was her turn to move Billy's stake. By this time Bertie had become afraid of Billy and he knew it. He loved to tease her by chasing her.

Bertie did not want to get close to Billy. She didn't want to appear a coward either. Bertie slowly started for Billy's stake.

Billy ignored her until she was almost to his stake. It looked like it was going to work. I was a little disappointed, but then Billy lowered his head and took after her.

She headed for the house on the run. When she reached the porch door she stopped. She turned to see where Billy was.

Since she hadn't pulled his stake up yet he had only run to the end of his rope.

Bertie stood panting and said, "I only remember coming through one of those fences." Then I could laugh. Bertie didn't laugh then but she laughs about it now.

It was soon after this that we unborrowed Billy. Dad took him back to the man who owned the lumberyard in Stapleton where he had borrowed him.

To this day I love goats and wish I could have one or two in my backyard.

## Chapter Eighteen

# I Get My Tonsils Out

It was hard to get eighteen-year-old girls to come up to teach school in the Sandhills, so far from civilization. Often we were left with the girls who couldn't get a school anyplace else. I remember one teacher as a mess. I'll call her Miss Doe.

One thing that stands out in my mind is the physical examination she gave each kid. I don't remember if the examination was her idea or if the county superintendent ordered all McPherson County kids to have a physical given by their teacher that year.

Miss Doe always carried a pencil, lead first, in her mouth. Most teachers carried their pencils in their hairdos or behind an ear. Miss Doe didn't have a hairdo and her ears may have been too far from her head to hold a pencil. Anyway she always carried her pencil in her mouth.

She called us up to her desk one at a time and told us to open our mouth. She then took the pencil out of her mouth and used it to hold down the kid's tongue, lead first. She looked in each kid's mouth, took the pencil out, wrote something on a piece of paper and put the pencil back in her mouth. Miss Doe repeated this process until she had given each of us eight kids a good physical.

That night she sent a paper home with each pupil describing his state of health. Bertie passed, but my paper told the folks I needed a tooth pulled and I also should have my tonsils out. This sounded exciting to me for I knew I would get to go to North Platte to have all that done.

I had already decided it might be fun to wear glasses and had convinced Mama I had trouble seeing. After recovering from the cold I caught from Miss Doe's pencil, Mama, Dad and I left the ranch early one morning before daylight for North Platte. We were traveling in our open air Ford touring car.

This was my day. I felt very special and wanted to make the most of it. I'd never been to a dentist before but I didn't think it could be too bad. Getting the glasses I knew would be fun. I had no idea how they would get my tonsils out and I wanted to get that over with first so I could enjoy the rest of the day. After all it was my day!

On the way to town I asked Mama if I could get my tonsils out first. Mama wisely said I should get that done last.

This was on a Saturday, so I wouldn't have to miss a day of school. The doctors, dentists and the glasses man worked on Saturdays in those days and one did not need an appointment. A potential patient just walked in. If the patient already knew what must be done, he told the doc. If the patient did not know, the doc figured it out on his own.

Our first stop was to the place to get my glasses. The man obliged me with a pair of gold-rimmed frames with plain glass for lenses.

Our next stop was the dentist, but I remember nothing of that.

Our third stop was Dr. Simms. I think I remember everything that happened in there. Mama told Dr. Simms I needed my tonsils taken out.

As I recall, there was just one room. It was upstairs in an old building in downtown North Platte. I don't remember any chairs, just a couple of stools and an old horsehair davenport that was raised at one end so when you laid down on it you were still half sitting up. There were some other things in one corner of the small room, but they are just a jumble in my mind. There was no other furniture, not even an examining table, though that may have been what the horsehair davenport was used for at times.

Dr. Simms had no nurse. He fixed a syringe full of liquid. There was a big needle on one end of the syringe. He laid the syringe on a low table. He got out a gadget with a two-inch wire loop on one end and what looked like a screwdriver handle on the other. He put this on the table with the syringe. Next he pulled the tallest stool over by the table with his two instruments on it. He sat down on the stool and pulled the shorter stool up between his knees and sat me on it. He gripped me tightly between his knees and told me to open my mouth. I did. That was my second mistake for the day. The first one was coming to North Platte. I wanted Mama and Dad to take me back to the ranch NOW!! It wasn't fun any more. It was getting mighty scary.

Mama had been standing by my shoulder, but the doctor told her to back up and stand by the wall. I think she was giving him too much help handling me.

Now there was just Dr. Simms and me and I still had my mouth open, but was watching him closely. He picked up the big syringe and stuck the needle in one of my tonsils. The tonsil started to grow numb. He did the same to the other tonsil.

Next he picked up the thing with the wire loop on it. He stuck that in my mouth and brought it out with one tonsil hanging on it. It wasn't so bad after all.

He got rid of that ugly piece of red meat and went in after the other tonsil. This time it hurt. I hollered but he didn't stop so I grabbed hold of both his hands. He couldn't move.

Here came Mama from her corner. I don't know how he got Mama back against the wall or how he got me to let go of his hands. He never let go of the grip he had on me with his knees, which was a good thing, for I would have been down on the street in a flash, no doubt with Mama after me.

What happened was the deadening had started to go out of that second tonsil by the time he started cutting it out with that wire loop.

Somehow the poor doctor finished the job, got the second tonsil out and laid me down on that funny-looking sofa. Mama sat on the end of it and we waited for Dad to finish his business in town and come up after us.

I remember Dad coming into the doctor's office. I guess Dr. Simms knew Dad as he said, "Hello, Bert. How are things?"

Dad answered, "Not so good, Doc. It's been a tough winter. How much do I owe you?"

Dr. Simms told him since times were hard, his fee would only be twenty-five dollars. Dad paid him and we got out of there.

The decision was made to stay all night in North Platte in a hotel. I knew it would be fun even if my throat was sore, and by now it hurt something awful.

We went down the street to the McCabe Hotel. I'll remember that hotel room as long as I live. It was so nice. The bed was all made and there was an electric light bulb on a long cord hanging from the ceiling right over the bed. All one had to do was turn a little knob on the end of the light bulb and you could see all over the room. At home if you wanted more light in another part of the room, you had to carry the lamp over.

Also at home, any member of the family who was sick got whatever he wanted to eat if it was possible to get it. My favorite thing to ask for when I was sick was an orange. If Dad or any of our neighbors were going to North Platte while I was sick, I got my orange. If not, I didn't. Here I was sick in North Platte, right where all the oranges came from.

I told Dad I wanted an orange. He went right out and got me one. Mama peeled it and gave me a section. I put it in my mouth and bit down. It burned like fire.

All I can recall of my wonderful first night in a hotel was being in bed and feeling terrible. Whenever I opened my eyes during the night I looked at that light bulb and thought, "How nice. Mama left the light on."

The weather turned very cold during the night. The folks still had to get me back to the ranch. They made a bed for me in the back seat of the old Ford.

Old Fords then did not have glass on the doors, but they had curtains made of a heavy black material. There were little windows of isinglass sewed in the curtains. That made it possible to peek out.

There were four curtains, one for each door. When the weather got real cold, the curtains were taken out from under the back seat (the gas tank was under the front seat) and snapped on the doors. They broke some of the wind, but didn't keep out any cold. It would be many years yet before they thought of putting heaters in cars.

Dad put the curtains on the car. I got in the back seat and lay down and they covered me up. The top cover was an old buffalo robe we always had in the car during the winter. We used it to throw over the car radiator to keep it from freezing if the car was going to be standing still any length of time. It also made a good lap robe while we were traveling. It was heavy but it was warm.

We were on our way to the ranch, at least a four-hour trip. My throat was awfully sore. I'd had nothing for pain since the deadening the doc shot in my tonsils the day before. I don't think they had pain pills yet. If so, Dr. Simms didn't know about them. It really didn't matter. My throat was too sore to swallow a pill.

It seemed to me the trip would never end. All I could do was lie under that buffalo robe and hurt. By now my throat hurt so much I wasn't even able to ask Dad how much further.

I thought about getting back to our house and being put to bed on the settee close to the big heater in the living room where Mama always put the kid that was sick. That was the only time we were ever babied. To this day I want to be babied when I'm sick.

It was late afternoon when we arrived home. The sun was shining in the west living room window and it looked so much better than the hotel room. Mama made the bed on the settee. They stirred up the fire in the big heater. I was home in bed on the settee by the nice warm fire but my throat still hurt.

It didn't feel any better the next morning, which was Monday. Bertie rode off to school alone.

I didn't figure I could live long feeling this bad. I remember plainly calling Mama in from the kitchen and asking her if I was going to die. She said, "Gracious no," and she was always right so I forgot about dying and started to get better.

I got well and was able to go back to school the next Monday. I was happy I only had one set of tonsils and would not have to go through that again.

The kids there were all eager to hear about my surgery and I was just as anxious to tell them. As I finished my story, one smart kid popped up and said, "Don'cha  know they'll grow back?"

That worried me for a long time, but it's been eighty years now. They haven't grown back yet.

# No Circus For Me

If my folks had let me go with the circus, I would be writing a different story.

The beautiful rolling Sandhills of western Nebraska are populated with cattle ranches ranging in size from ten sections to forty sections. (One section is 640 acres.) I was raised on a ten-section ranch in McPherson County. There were six in our family not counting the dogs, cats and other pets. Our ranch, known as the Ten Bar Ranch or the Snyder place was twelve miles west of Tryon. Tryon, the county seat and the only town in McPherson County, boasted a population of nearly a hundred hardy souls.

It was as a small kid on this ranch that I dreamed of going with a circus. Mama had taken my older brother, Miles, my younger sister, Bertie, and me to see a circus. I must have been about six years old at the time.

I remember the excitement, all the wonderful animals, the great looking people who did all those great things. I went home thinking that I had to live like that and be a part of it all. That is, of course, when I grew up.

From then on I tried the things I saw the circus performers do. I tried walking on my hands. It looked easy, but I couldn't do it. I found if I got close to a wall, faced it and kicked my feet in the air as I put my hands on the floor, my feet could hit the wall and I could stand there. This strengthened my arm and shoulder muscles for what was to come later and it was fun.

I remembered seeing a lady trick rider, a beautiful lady on a beautiful white

*Billie learning to walk a wire*

horse. I pictured myself being her.

As I had a horse and saddle handy at all times, I started trick riding, not knowing that I needed a trained horse and a trick riding saddle. I used my old cow pony and my little old kid's saddle. I reached the point where I could stand up in the saddle if the horse just walked. Any faster and I had to slide down into the saddle or jump off.

I was about nine or ten when the folks took us to the county fair and rodeo. There I saw a girl do a tight-wire act. That looked easy.

On our way home I asked Dad if he could fix me a tight-wire like that girl had so I could learn to walk it.

He answered "I'll see."

I knew that meant he would do it.

He used a half-inch cable about sixty feet long. He tied one end to a tree and the other end to a post in the pig pen fence. He stretched it tight with his wire stretcher. The cable was about four feet off the ground, which was a good thing as I spent most of the rest of that fall climbing the tree to get on the wire and jumping off when I lost my balance. At first I only took three or four steps before I had to jump.

During the winter Dad used that cable to pull the haystacks over on to the hay-sled to feed the cattle. My tight-wire came down. It was too cold by then to practice.

Dad put the cable back up the next spring. That summer I got further between climb-ups and jump-offs. I never did get to the point that I could walk the whole sixty feet. I do have a snapshot that Mama took. I'm about halfway across, but leaning far to the left and nearly ready to jump.

I still couldn't walk more than a step or two on my hands. I hadn't mastered trick riding or the tight-wire. I had made more progress on the wire than I had trick riding, but felt sure I could do it all. I wasn't quite grown up yet. I had a few years left to practice.

It was about this time an old cowboy friend of Dad's named Sandy came to visit. None of the rest of the family had ever seen Sandy before. Dad hadn't seen him since his cowboy days. We knew Sandy was a very special friend of Dad's so we all tried to act in a way Dad would be proud of us.

One day I was washing dishes in the kitchen. Mama was also in the kitchen. Sandy walked in for a drink of water. I guess he thought he would try to talk to that awkward, shy kid.

He asked, "What do you intend to do when you grow up?"

I told him I was going to travel with a circus.

Mama was horrified.

As soon as Sandy went back outside Mama gave me the worst scolding of my life. The very idea, a daughter of hers going with a circus. I was never to let her hear me tell that to anyone again.

Well, I saw to it that she was never in hearing distance when I told people what I intended to do when I grew up. I never mentioned going with a circus in front of either of the folks again. I did keep on with the acrobatics and the tight rope walking. I gave up on the trick riding. I'm sure Midget, my horse, was happy about that. Now she didn't have to stop so often and wait for me to get back on.

Many years later a circus came to North Platte. Dad rounded up all his kids and grandkids and treated us to a day at the circus. I remember telling him that if he had let me go with the circus when I wanted to, I would be getting us all in free. Dad chuckled. He did like circuses, but he didn't want his daughter traveling with one.

*More pictures of Billie practicing for the circus.*

**Bertie and Me**

# God In The Sandhills

When my brother Miles was past eighty, I asked him if he believed in God. He said, "Bill, you can't ride these hills as long as I have and not believe in God."

He could not have given me a more reassuring answer. Those words came to me many times the night I sat watching his breathing slow to a stop. I took one last look at his quiet face and knew he was up there where the hills are always green and never covered with snow.

Miles lived most of his ninety-one years on that ranch in the sandhills. Mother had gone to her sisters, thirty-five miles south of the ranch for Miles's birth. Two weeks later she carried baby Miles home on horseback. There he lived and helped Dad work the ranch for the next twenty years, at which time he took five years off to see some of the world and do his hitch in the army.

After his five-year vacation he went back to the ranch. That's where he wanted to be. He worked the ranch with Dad until Dad retired, then the ranch was his and he raised his family there. He lived there until he died.

I'll try to let you see why he gave me the answer he did. Much of his work was riding the many pastures on the ranch, checking and counting the cattle, making sure the windmills were working and the tanks were full of water. The many miles of barbed-wire fences had to be up and cattle tight.

Miles would saddle his horse at the barn and head for the pasture he would work that day. He was soon out of sight of the ranch buildings. There was just

Miles, his horse, the cattle he was looking over, jackrabbits, ground squirrels, field mice and birds of many kinds.

The cows that weren't eating were lying down so peaceful and quiet they seemed to be meditating. The ground squirrels and field mice were in no hurry. They knew they were safe and in no danger. The silence was only broken by the birds giving their native call to welcome whoever was there to their home.

There might be some horses in the next pasture. If so, there would be one more broken silence. One of those horses would give a friendly whinny to the horse Miles was riding.

Some pastures had lakes. There would be a flock of ducks or some other water birds near the center. A long legged killdeer could be running along the shore of the lake. If she had a nest nearby she would run with a big limp and drag one wing as though it was broken. She would be repeating two bird words, "Kill Deer," over and over to be sure of getting Miles's attention and leading him away from her nest.

Miles might see a leery coyote on a hill not too far off. She no doubt would have a den of pups near by and was standing watch over them.

God feels very close in a setting such as this.

*Miles and his horse Mustard*

## Chapter Twenty-One

# ANGELS ON HORSEBACK

Miles felt God in other ways. Once his horse stepped in a gopher hole. The horse fell and threw Miles to the ground, knocking him unconscious. Miles landed in an anthill and was covered with red biting ants. He regained consciousness, not knowing how long he had lain there. His horse was not hurt and stood nearby waiting for him to get up. Miles was able to brush off the ants, get on his horse and ride home.

Many incidents like this happened. All of the saddle horses must have been used to having an angel riding behind the saddle.

There was another time an angel was on a horse with Miles. I only heard Mama tell this story but she told it many times.

Miles was seven. He was to ride a three-year-old gentle mare that was being broke for a kid's saddle horse. Dad was getting his horse ready to ride, but hadn't saddled him yet. Miles was to lead his saddled horse, Midget, out the barnyard gate, get on and head for the meadow. Dad would follow in a few minutes.

Suddenly Dad heard the sound of horse's hooves. He looked up and saw Midget on a high run. Miles was hanging head down against the horse's right shoulder, his feet up. Dad's horse was wearing only a bridle but Dad leaped on him bareback and took after Miles and Midget. Before Dad could reach them, Miles dropped to the ground. The horse kept on running.

Dad jumped off his horse and picked up Miles. He discovered Miles was a little stunned, but otherwise the only damage was to his overall pocket. It was torn wide open.

Miles told Dad he was climbing on Midget when something spooked her. She took off running and he wound up caught on the saddle horn with his head downhill. Then he fell to the ground.

There were times people thought God was not all that near. A hired man named Fritz was mowing hay with a mower pulled by a team of horses. Dad was mowing a ways behind Fritz. He looked up to see Fritz standing by his mower holding the reins to the team tight in one hand and his hat in his other hand. He was fanning his fanny for all he was worth.

When Dad drew near he heard Fritz yelling over and over, "HELL AIN'T HALF MILE FROM HERE."

Fritz had mowed into a bumblebee nest and many angry bees had stung him through the holes in the mower seat. It was a good thing the bees attacked Fritz instead of the horses. Had that happened the team would surely have run away.

When there was a runaway team of horses, especially one pulling a mowing-machine, they said, "ALL HELL BROKE LOOSE." The ranch must have furnished guardian angels for the hired help. It took an old-timer angel to have the bees sting Fritz instead of the horses.

The guardian angels were busy during haying season. Horses pulled the machines. Many horses only worked during haying and some were not very gentle and would easily spook and run away. Lots of machines were broken or torn up, but no one on our ranch was ever hurt badly enough to need a doctor. Which reminds me-no one carried insurance and I never heard of a lawsuit by hired help.

I think back on it now and wonder how the angels worked it. When things got tough, did they call on a near-by angel for help or did they have back-ups like our policemen do now?

Then there were two little girls who had the run of the ranch. The only thing they were not allowed to do was climb the windmill and get on the platform by the wheel even if the windmill was shut off. If they did this and the wind should change the big wheel would swing with the wind. The girls might be knocked off and fall in the tank of water and drown.

It seemed the folks thought we could recover from anything but drowning, and we did, thanks to our angels.

We were always trying new and different things just to see how interesting things would get. Once Bertie got the worst of it with her angel saving her when she and I went skating.

There was a pond a short distance from the house. In real cold weather the ice was thick and Bertie and I liked to go skating.

A wire fence ran through the ice at the south end of the lake. It was the right height to sit on and fasten our skates to our shoes. Dad had told us not to sit on it anymore as it made the fence so slack a critter could get over it when the lake thawed.

When we got to the ice that fence was so handy to sit on, I thought, "One more time won't hurt."

I sat on it and started to put on my skates. Bertie gave me a look and said, "Bill, Dad said we are not to do that anymore."

As I got up, she sat down where I had been sitting.

I didn't like that so I grabbed the fence and gave it a jerk. Bertie fell forward, striking her forehead hard on the ice. She got up and headed for the house on the run with me right with her. Fortunately we had been fussing instead of putting on our skates and we were free to run. We left our skates on the ice.

By the time we got to the house, Bertie had a huge lump on one corner of her forehead. She laid down on the lounge and went into a deep sleep. Mama watched her very closely until she woke up, which seemed forever to me.

It seemed every time Bertie cried, I got spanked. This time I didn't. If Mama had only spanked or even scolded me I would have felt better. Mama simply ignored me and wouldn't listen to what I wanted to say.

I waited it out and Bertie woke up and was O.K. Her angel did a good job that time.

## Chapter Twenty-Two

# NAMING THE ANIMALS

We named everything on the ranch except the cattle. There were several hundred of them. We named the milk cows, but the cattle herd was into the hundreds.

The two milk cows I liked best were Old Tex and Little Tex. Little Tex was a calf from Old Tex and I made a skimmer calf out of her, that is, I taught her to drink milk from a bucket. A new born calf's first instinct is to put his nose up and start searching for that thing the milk comes out of. This calf was so small she didn't look like she'd ever amount to much.

Dad gave Little Tex to me, but only to claim, which meant when she went to market the money went into the business. It was fun just to have something to claim.

I taught Little Tex how a skimmer calf drinks. I milked a few inches into a bucket and took it over to her. She smelled the warm milk and stuck her nose up in the air.

I cupped my hand over her nose, put three fingers in her mouth and pushed with all of my strength to get her nose into the warm milk. She sucked some milk up through my fingers.

*Billie and her pet milk cow*
*"Little Tex"*

As soon as I took my fingers out of her mouth, her head came straight up looking for his mama's teat.

I kept pushing her head back into the bucket until she got enough milk in her belly to tide her over to her next feeding.

It took three days of this before the little skimmer calf put her head into the bucket to drink. From then she was fed only skimmed milk. Thus the name of skimmer calf. Skimmer calves develop a potbelly and other signs like anything deprived of its mother. They are true orphans.

One time Dad came in and told Bertie and me the old sow pig had had babies. Bertie and I ran out to the pigpen. There were about a dozen cute little pigs. The old sow was very gentle and didn't mind us picking her babies up. We took our time and carefully named each little pig while mama pig laid there doing a contented and happy grunt.

The next time we went out to play with the cute little pigs we couldn't tell which was which since they were all black and looked just alike.

Our sweet old shepherd dog was Towser. He would sit out on the knoll west of the house and watch for Bertie and me when it was time for us to come home from school.

The old tomcat was named Tom. He sat on the kitchen sill and looked in.

*Bertie and her pet chicken, Pete. Chicken coop to the right and the dog houses to the rear.*

Wish I had a picture of that. I don't remember Old Tom ever being in the house. Towser could come in sometimes if it was real cold outside.

The billy goat was named Billy.

Bertie had an old pet hen she called Pete.

Naming the horses was fun. We let our imagination go to work for us. They were named when they were colts and many times they were named according to their color.

Once we got into spices. We had a Ginger, a Mustard and a Pepper. They were each the color of the spice they were named for. We all had a hand in naming the horses. Mama named two colts. She named one Taffy and the other one Penuche. Mama had a sweet tooth. There again each colt resembled the color of candy he was named for.

We even got into the army. We had a team of workhorses named Major and Colonel.

The team Mama drove on the hay rake was named Jake and Geronimo. Geronimo was named for an Indian. Mama loved that team and wouldn't drive any other team.

The old sleepy stacker team I drove on my first job in the hayfield when I was six years old was named Knute and Charlie. I don't know where their names came from, but I'll never forget them. Old Knute was white and Old Charlie was bay.

*Dad driving the mower with Major and Colonel*

That was over eighty years ago and I can't help but wonder where their bones are now. Probably enjoying their rest some place. I hope so.

Mama had a horse she loved to ride. He was high-spirited but he was also gentle and very affectionate. He loved to rub his nose on her shoulder. He was a beautiful sorrel named Jeff.

Way back then women wore long skirts, even to ride horseback. The riding skirts were of heavy material but were divided, that is, they had two legs. They were still ankle length. Horses had to be broke special for a woman to ride. The man breaking the horse took a blanket or wore a pair of chaps with legs unbuckled to get the horse used to the riding skirt flapping around his sides. They sure don't have that problem now. That is good.

Dad had three very special horses that no one rode but Dad. The first one that I remember was a gray horse named Dewey. Dad caught him from a herd of wild horses about the time Admiral George Dewey was the hero of the time. Commodore Dewey had sunk the entire Spanish fleet in Manila Bay on May 1, 1898. It was during the Spanish-American War, after which he became Admiral Dewey. So Dad named his horse Dewey.

After Dad broke Dewey to ride he turned out to be one of the best horses Dad ever had. The whole family loved Dewey. Dewey was an old horse by the time Bertie and I remember him. We were proud of the fact that he had been named for an admiral. We didn't know what an admiral was but we knew it was someone very important. None of the family ate any supper the night Old Dewey died.

I don't remember much about Dad's second special horse. He was a beautiful sorrel color with very thick silver mane and tail, which may have been where he got the name of Silver. I just remember Silver was a beautiful horse and no one rode him but Dad. We kids were to be careful round him, never go in the stall with him and stay far back from his heels. Dad said Silver was a stallion and couldn't be trusted. He had a special stall in the barn and he was treated with much care and respect.

The third horse of Dad's special horses I remember well. His name was Antelope. His coloring resembled that of an antelope. He was a big, strong, handsome horse. I loved to see Dad ride him. I thought they were a great pair.

*Some of our horses. Antelope is the first one on the left. Notice the pile of ice to the left chipped from the water tank.*

They seemed to compliment each other. Antelope stood out in a herd of horses because of his unusual coloring.

I used to like to show a snapshot of our herd of horses to someone who knew the horses. They immediately started naming the horses they recognized. The first one named was always Antelope.

We each had our special saddle horse. Bertie's horse was named Snip. She was a big, gentle, white horse. It was quite a job for five-year-old Bertie to climb up on old Snip. At home in the mornings when we went out to go to school there was always Dad or Miles or a hired man to throw her on old Snip. Once on she was safe for Snip didn't make any more moves than she needed to.

*Bertie ready to get on Chief, Billie on Midget, and a friend at the local rodeo gathering.*

Midget was my horse's name. Dad gave her to me when I was a baby and Midget was a baby colt. We were both girls. Midget carried me to school from first through eighth grade. I also rode her in a few horse races. Each year the county fair and local rodeo had a ladies horse race. There were always two regulars for that race, me on Midget and Helen Trego on her fast beautiful brown horse named Chief. Helen and Chief always came in first. I always came in second on Midget.

If there happened to be one or two more in the race that day, they, of course, came in third and fourth.

Nellie had a horse named Dinah. Nellie was very small. She was under five feet tall and weighed less than a hundred pounds. Dinah was a very small horse. She was a bald-faced bay, a pretty color, but she looked like a stick horse with four legs. She was all heart though and could carry Nellie's ninety some pounds and keep up with the rest of us on bigger horses.

Miles had two very pretty buckskin-colored horses that he broke for himself to work cattle on. The big one was named Turk and the smaller one named Mustard. They were both skittish and had to be handled just so. He told me never to try to ride either one. One day I tried to ride Turk and found out why he had told me not to ride him. I had trouble for a few days trying to walk so it didn't show where I was hurt. Turk threw me before I could get clear on.

As time went on, we used fewer horses to run the ranch. A pickup could fill in for a couple of saddle horses. It was easy to hop in a pickup and drive out to check the windmills. Dad had gotten too old to break his own horses. When he needed another saddlehorse, he bought it already broken. These horses came already named.

After I left the ranch, I remember Dad had a Nibbs and a Casey. They were beautiful horses, but their names didn't mean anything to me.

## Chapter Twenty-Three

# CATTLE RUSTLING

I'm starting this story with an article from the *McPherson County History Book*.

*AUGUST 23, 1923 John Hunter, who lives north of here (Tryon), was arrested for stealing 38 head of cattle from the Rufe Haney pasture, 12 miles west of Tryon on August 3. It is said that he drove the cattle to a ranch on Birdwood Creek, where he rebranded them and disfigured the Haney brand, but the work was easily detected.*

*After his arrest, he became very ill at the jail in North Platte. It was thought for awhile that he would not recover. He was taken to the hospital. The last report we had, he is some better. It is thought at this writing he will recover. His illness is said to be caused by drinking too much "HOOCH". R. E. Glenn of North Platte was arrested this week in connection with the cattle stealing. September 27, 1923 Hunter pleaded guilty. October 4th he was sentenced to four years in the state Penitentiary.*

The morning started out like any other morning on our ranch during haying. Miles, Bertie and I fed the chickens, slopped the hogs and milked the cows. Mama cooked breakfast. Dad brought the herd of horses in from horse pasture and corralled them.

After breakfast Dad, Miles and the hired man went out to the corral and caught the teams to use in the hayfield that morning. The rest of the horses went back to the pasture. It was my job to bring the horses in again at noon. I liked that job and knew how to do it. But today was going to be different.

Dad and Mama were very quiet during breakfast. We kids knew better than to ask any questions. After a fast meal Dad went out to the corral and caught his best saddle horse, saddled up in a hurry and headed north. Miles and the hired man caught their teams and went out to mow hay. Any other time Dad would have been with them. Dad didn't say where he was going.

Bertie and I couldn't figure out what Dad was up to, so we finally asked Mama, as she seemed very upset. She said it was none of our business. It seemed Bertie and I would never be old enough for things to be 'any of our business.'

Mama fixed an extra good dinner that day, home canned beef in its own gravy, my very favorite meal. I sure wanted to get those horses in and be at dinner on time.

I had just gotten on my horse and had ridden past the windmill when I met Dad and two of our neighbors, Bird Huffman and Charlie Daly. I didn't know this at the time, but as Dad gathered the horses that morning he noticed a herd of cattle had recently been driven out of the Rufe Haney pasture.

Rufe's pasture joined our horse pasture. It had rained the night before, just enough to preserve the cattle tracks in the sand. Dad knew that Rufe Haney had not taken any cattle from his pasture that summer. The cattle had been stolen. Dad knew what had to be done and FAST. They had to trail those cattle and catch the rustlers.

Dad needed help. He couldn't call for it on the county party line. That might alert the whole country and this had to be kept quiet. He got on his best horse and hightailed it for help. He came back with Bird Huffman and Charley Daly. Huffman's ranch was nine miles north of ours and Daly's was six miles north.

Dad rode up to me and said in a stern voice, "Bill, bring in every horse in the pasture." As a rule, I only brought in the afternoon workhorses. If I saw a saddle horse or two off at a distance I didn't bother to go after them.

The first mile of the horse pasture from the barn was flat, then it got hilly, lots of places for horses to hide. Today I found almost all the horses in a bunch behind the first hill. All except ol' Turk, a big strong saddle horse, one of our best.

Turk was a long ways to the south. He was a loner and hard to drive. I judged the distance and thought of the good beef and gravy Mama was putting on the table for dinner. I thought to myself that Dad surely didn't mean for me to bring in Turk. We never used him in the hayfield. I brought the rest of the horses in on the run.

Dad was there to shut the corral gate when I got them in. I told him, "I got'em all but ol' Turk. He was way over south."

Dad was unusually cross. He said, "I told you to bring in every horse in the pasture. Now go back and get Turk."

I went back.

I had a hard time with him. He kept trying to break back and get into the hills. After several attempts, ol' Turk gave up and headed for the corral. Dad was there to close the gate on him. Dad and I went to the house. Bird and Charlie and the rest of the family had just finished eating. There was some meat and gravy left. I cleaned that up in a hurry.

Bertie and I sure wondered what was up, but we knew it was a darned good time to keep quiet. Dad, Bird and Charlie went out to the barn where they had tied their horses. Of course, Bertie and I followed and climbed up on the eight-foot corral fence, our grandstand seat for seeing what was going on. We saw Dad catch three of our best saddle horses, Ol' Turk among them.

Bird and Charlie took their saddles off their horses and put them on two of the horses Dad had just brought from the corral. Dad took his saddle off the horse he'd ridden that morning, put it on ol' Turk and cinched it up. He lifted the left stirrup up, hooked it over the saddle horn and secured his rifle in the rifle holder. He was already wearing his six shooter. The three men swung up on their horses and headed south.

We knew we'd better worry.

Later that afternoon a man we had never seen before rode up to our barn on the run. His horse was so hot it had white lather on its shoulders. Mama went out to meet him, Bertie and me right behind her.

Bertie and I were hanging pretty close to Mama by now. The rider was sweating and he asked for Bert (Dad). Mama said Bert wasn't home and she didn't know where he had gone.

Mama knew Dad had gone after a cow thief, but she didn't know this man. For all she knew, he might be one of the thieves and after Dad.

After the man calmed down some, he introduced himself, saying he was Rufe Haney's hired man and Mr. Haney was short thirty-eight head of cattle. Then Mama told him Dad and the others were already on the trail. Mama wouldn't tell Bertie and me any more than she told Haney's hired man.

Miles and our hired man came in from the hayfield. We did the evening chores. Mama wouldn't leave the house. She stayed within hearing distance of the phone.

Bertie and I had hardly taken our eyes off Mama after Dad rode off. We even slept with her that night.

Things were very quiet around our place until the next afternoon when our phone gave our ring: a long, three shorts and a long. Mama answered the phone in a hurry and I could see her face relax as she listened.

Dad was on the phone calling from some ranch near North Platte. He said they found the cattle. Mama wouldn't give us any details. That wasn't important to me then. My dad was safe and would soon be home again!

Dad, Mr. Daly and Mr. Huffman rode into our place late that night. We were all in bed, but when the three men walked in we were up in no time to hear all about it.

The thieves had leased a pasture from a rancher near North Platte. The rancher did not know the cattle were stolen. Dad asked the names of the men who left the cattle. The names were not the names he expected to hear. He asked for a description.

The description of one of the rustlers fit our handsome young unmarried neighbor, John Hunter. He was the one the men suspected all along.

John Hunter was well-known and well-liked. All the gals in the Sandhills were in love with him, including eleven-year-old me. They had to catch him red-handed and they did.

We were broken-hearted. John Hunter couldn't steal cattle. After all we saw him at every sandhill rodeo, Roman riding with one foot on each of his two beautiful white horses. He had stayed all night at our place many times and helped us do the evening chores.

Mama started a fire in the kitchen range and cooked a big meal for the men who hadn't had much to eat since they left the day before.

*John Hunter Roman riding on his horses*

We heard how they had finally found Haney's thirty-eight head of cattle at the Rosedale ranch several miles north of North Platte, then called the Lincoln County sheriff giving the description of the two men who had left the cattle at the Rosedale ranch. They also gave John Hunter's name.

In a short time the sheriff had arrested John and his partner in crime and had them in jail. Back then, justice worked much faster

*John Hunter visiting our ranch.*
*Back row: Nellie, Mama*
*Middle row: Dad, a neighbor, John Hunter*
*Front row: Bertie, a neighbor kid.*

than it does now. John was in the Nebraska State Penitentiary within two months of his arrest.

We were very sad about John being in the pen. My eighteen-year-old sister, Nellie, was devastated. I remember Nellie made a trip to Lincoln (where the pen was). She asked Mama if it would be all right if she went to see John. Mama said, "Yes," but Nellie didn't have the nerve to go. She didn't know what to say to him. She said, "I couldn't ask him how he liked it there."

None of us ever saw him again. He did his time, got out and came back to North Platte.

The story goes that he learned how to bootleg while in the pen. He was released in 1927 and came back to the sandhills to start his own business. Bootlegging was a moneymaking deal during the twenties and early thirties until probation was voted out.

John Hunter was big news around North Platte until some time in 1931 when no one seemed to know where he was. It was a big mystery. Did things get too hot around here and he had to leave the area or had he been killed? Being killed was the most popular. Getting killed was not unusual for a bootlegger in those days.

The years went by, but we still didn't know what happened to John until 1938 when someone talked and told where John was buried.

John's bones were found buried in a barn a few miles south of Maxwell. We saw a picture of his bones in the North Platte *Evening Telegraph* at the time they were found. I remember looking at that picture and thinking what a handsome face once was formed over those cheekbones.

## Chapter Twenty-four

# WE ARE BAPTIZED

**O**verlooking the Dismal River just sixteen miles north of our ranch sits a beautiful white frame building with a small cross on the front peak of the roof. It is the All Saints Episcopal Church. It is called the Eclipse Church, getting its name from a long ago post office that once sat on that spot.

The church, with the growing cemetery in back, has a well kept barbed wire fence around it to keep the cattle and horses from messing things up. It's a beautiful, quiet scene, with no other buildings in sight. The story and history of the Eclipse Episcopal Church and cemetery is very fascinating. I hope someone writes it some day soon.

The Episcopal Bishop from Omaha came to Eclipse once a year and baptized all the people within a hundred miles - at least all those who wanted baptized or needed it or had been missed the year before. Bishop Beacher was very serious about seeing that people, especially kids, were baptized.

A friend told me of one occasion when the bishop drove through the sandhills, baptizing people at their homes. A mother wanted her kids baptized. She expected Bishop Beacher to stop but she had also warned her kids to be leery of strangers because a stranger might steal a kid.

Bishop Beacher drove into their yard. By the time he reached the house, the mother couldn't find any of her kids. The kids had seen the strange car drive in and they all hid out. Their mother was determined to have her family baptized but she

*Eclipse Church as it looks today. Notice the cemetery to the right.*

had to find them first. She soon found the girls. It took longer to find her son. He was well hidden in the barn.

I'm sure Bishop Beacher then drove the three or four miles to the next ranch and experienced the same thing.

A neighbor lady, Ruby Huffman, called Mama and told her Bishop Beacher would be coming to the Eclipse church soon. Mama had three kids that needed to be baptized: Miles, Billie and Bertie. Sister Nellie had been baptized in the Baptist Church in Maxwell the year before when she was going to high school.

When Bishop Beacher came, he held Episcopal services. People met at the Eclipse Church and spent the biggest part of the day there. Each family brought their specialty in food. At noon there was a feast that only those ranch women could accomplish, and on their cow-chip-burning kitchen ranges at that.

As people arrived they walked through the cemetery. The first grave, the grave that started the cemetery, was an unknown baby. The stone simply reads: "UNKNOWN BABY 1890."

There are many graves of babies and young children in the lot. There are also graves of some desperados, but mostly graves of just good people that the visitors knew during their lifetime.

After the walk through the cemetery, neighbors visited neighbors, some who hadn't seen each other for a year. The men took care of the financial church business. The women lay out the feast.

After we ate, things were cleaned up and everyone went into the church for the services and the baptisms.

I remember nothing of the services. The picture I have in mind is Dad, Mama, Miles, Bertie and me kneeling on something and Bishop Beacher baptizing we three kids. Oh yes, Ruby Huffman was kneeling with us. She was our Godmother.

After the services were over, everyone headed for home. We had sixteen miles to drive in our old Ford over those sandy, rutty, twisty hilly roads. Some of the hills were high enough that the whole family except the driver had to jump out and push the car over them.

There were many gates to be opened and driven through, but with a driver, a gate opener, and enough people to push the car if it got stuck in the sand, we got home in time to change into our work clothes and get the cows in, milk them and do the other nightly chores.

During the drive home from the church I had plenty of time to think over the whole day. The heaviest thought in my mind was that the whole country surely wouldn't go to all that trouble just to make kids think that there was a God. I was pretty sure now there really was a God and I would have to watch the things I did and said.

Then I thought about all the graves up behind the church. There was a special feeling there that I couldn't explain.

In later years on visiting Eclipse, I experienced the same feeling, realizing it as a feeling of peace. Many others I've talked to experience the same feeling. Now in the year 2002, the beautiful white church is still there. It still has no electricity, just kerosene lamps on brackets along each wall. The cemetery is much larger. They extended the barbed-wire fence to include another acre of land for future graves.

I attended a funeral there a few years ago and saw a startled, striped garter snake scurrying away as the crowd approached the open grave.

The Snyder family has a very sad story that involves the Eclipse cemetery. Four years ago my handsome seventeen-year-old great, great nephew, Brandon Blake was killed in a car accident in McPherson County very near his home. His mother and dad, Janelle and Kim Blake, and his brother Arlis wanted to have the services for Brandon on Sunday as many of his friends were away from home during the rest of the week.

The funeral was held in the large gymnasium of the Tryon high school. After the services, the mile-long funeral procession left Tryon for the Eclipse cemetery, a thirty-mile drive. Now there is a narrow paved road over the Sandhills and no gates. It was late in the afternoon before the long line of cars arrived and found parking around the cemetery.

Thirteen of Brandon's friends walked with the casket to the grave and the raw mound of dirt beside it. Young pallbearers carried the casket and set it on the lowering device. The many young girls who called Brandon a friend came and put flowers on top of the casket.

There were four throw-ropes stretched across the grave. Eight of the pallbearers stepped up, picked up the ropes and lifted the casket while the lowering device was removed. The boys then slowly lowered their friend into his grave and dropped the ropes on top of the casket.

Hesitating before the open grave, Brandon's brother Arlis stood quietly until a cousin, Tyler Neal, said, "Whenever you're ready, Bud." Arlis threw in the first shovelful of dirt and then the other young men came with their shovels and slowly, sadly filled the grave.

Brandon's friends stayed with him to the last.

## Chapter Twenty-five

# Warts

Kids in country schools were stuck with one teacher for the whole school year. If you liked her, fine, if not, too bad. This next story is of a teacher we loved, the only teacher we had for two years. She boarded with us. Her name was Grace Spence, but we called her Miss Spence.

Miss Spence got rid of my warts. I had several warts on one hand. I didn't like having those warts. Miss Spence told me she was going to get rid of them for me. I didn't believe it then and I don't believe it now, but it happened.

It was recess time and the other kids were out in the yard playing. Miss Spence closed the schoolhouse door. She had a piece of string in her hand. She took me over by a window, opened it and crawled out.

She had me reach my wart hand out, but I was not to look to see what she was doing. She held my hand but I couldn't see. Soon she let go of my hand, crawled back through and closed the window.

I stood there wondering, "What the heck?"

She told me not to ask questions or to tell anyone.

By now recess time was up. Miss Spence rang the bell and the kids came in. We took our seats and finished that day of school.

In a few days the warts were gone. I don't remember them getting smaller or how they left, but they were gone. My hand was completely free of warts.

Miss Spence asked to look at my hand one day, so I asked her what she did to get rid of my warts. She said she had tied knots in that piece of string, one for each wart on my hand, then buried the string. It all had to be secret or it wouldn't work. That was why she had to go out the window, so none of the kids in the schoolyard would see her. It was also the reason I could not tell anyone what she had done.

I never had another wart.

## Chapter Twenty-Six

# BUTCHERING

The whole family always anticipated the time in the fall when it was cold enough to butcher our first beef of the winter. There would be two more beeves butchered before the weather warmed up in the spring. We were beef eaters.

Dad felt that to amount to anything one had to eat lots of beef. And that included the kids, especially the kids. When we went to school, he told Mama to send us each with a steak in our dinner buckets. We had never heard of a lunch. It was either breakfast, dinner or supper. At school it was dinner, even if we ate it out of a pound tobacco pail.

One morning Dad said, "You kids better take a frying pan to school, then you can heat up your steaks." I stuck a big frying pan in my saddle sack along with my dinner bucket and bottle of drinking water.

That frying pan just fit the top of our pot-bellied heater at school. From then on we heated up our steaks, that is, if we had time and felt like it. Otherwise we ate them cold. To this day I like a good steak almost as well cold as hot.

As I write this I can't recall ever taking that frying pan home to wash it. After we warmed our steaks we set the pan to cool, then hung it on a nail back where all the kids hung their wraps and kept their dinner pails.

All that beef and the dirty frying pan seem to have done us no harm. Bertie and I are still going strong.

Butchering Day. Dad had put a two or three-year-old heifer in the barn the night before. He had selected her a few weeks back and penned her up. He fed her all the hay she would eat. Being penned up she wouldn't be able to run or walk off any fat.

When Dad and my brother Miles were ready to start butchering, Dad opened the barn door. He had his rifle in his hands and shot the critter as soon as she looked up. Her heels were secured, one to each end of a singletree. This spread her heels about three feet apart.

There was a block and tackle fastened to the peak of the barn. The pulley on the big rope was lowered to the ground and fastened to the singletree. The animal was pulled high enough so Dad and Miles could skin her, starting at the back knees.

After she was skinned and her insides were drained out into a big tub, they wrapped a sheet around the carcass and pulled it to the tip of the barn. It was left there to cool all night.

The liver, heart, and sweetbreads were saved from what was in the tub. We had liver for supper. The tongue was cut out of the mouth and the brains taken from the skull. The heart and tongue were boiled and pickled for summer eating. The brains were scrambled with eggs and eaten as a delicacy for breakfast the following morning.

By then the carcass had cooled down enough for Dad and Miles to finish and get the meat ready for the meat house. They lowered the carcass down to where it could be worked on with knives and saws. Dad and Miles cut

*Miles and Dad butchering a heifer. Notice the singletree attached to the block and tackle.*

and sawed it into quarters. The two front quarters were much smaller than the two hindquarters. All four legs were cut off at the knees. The lower legs were thrown to the pigs and the chickens.

Dad carried the quarters into the meat house and hung them through the knee on large meat hooks. There was a big strong table in the meat house. Dad took the quarter and laid it on the table. With a very sharp knife and a hand meatsaw, he sliced the meat and brought in for our next meal. We ate whatever we came to on the quarter Dad was working on.

We kids never knew one cut of meat from another. It was all just beefsteak to us. Sometimes it had bones in it and sometimes it didn't. When the steaks had no bones, we had boiled potatoes and gravy, or if we were short of potatoes, we ate the gravy on baking powder biscuits. That steak (we know it now as round steak) with potatoes and gravy or biscuits and gravy was a favorite of the whole family.

The big roasts were always good, but when it came time for the boiled meat, we kids cut way back on our meat eating.

When it was really cold and the meat was frozen solid, Dad carried the whole hindquarter into the kitchen and lay it on the oilcloth on the long dining table. The meat could be sliced very thin when it was that frozen.

Mama put a couple of large iron skillets on the range. Using butter for cooking oil, Mama fried the thin slices of meat as Dad sliced them off. Each kid stood by Mama with a big slice of homemade bread brushed generously with melted butter waiting for her to pile a couple of layers of thin, hot juicy beef on his/her slice of bread.

As we finished eating that open sandwich we stepped up, picked up another slice of bread, brushed it generously with hot butter and waited for Mama to pile the meat on again.

It was surprising how many of those sandwiches four kids and two adults could eat. No one sat down. We just stood around the range and ate while watching Dad thin-slice beef and Mama cook it.

We called those Bread'n' Meat Suppers. They were the favorite of everyone. There was no table to clean off, no dishes to do. Mama cleaned the stove and skillets. Dad carried what was left of the beef quarter back to the meat house. You might say the kids had an evening off. We often asked the folks if we could have a bread 'n meat supper, but we could only do it when the meat was frozen enough to be sliced very thin.

Mama canned many quarts of beef for summer meals during haying. The meat was cut into small pieces, packed in quart glass jars and sealed very tight with a lid. The jars were then lined up in a large wash boiler. The boiler was filled with water.

The next thing was to keep the kitchen range very hot. This was done by a girl kid poking cow chips in the front of the stove. Another girl kid carried baskets full of chips in from the chip pile and carried out buckets of ashes to dump in the pigpen.

Life on a ranch wasn't always exciting for a couple of little girls. In fact it could be down right boring at times, but there was always something to look forward to. Bread 'n' Meat suppers was one of them.

## Chapter Twenty-seven

# HELPING HAND CLUB

*Keep Climbing, Though The Hills Be Rugged*, was, and still is, the slogan for The Helping Hand Club. This tough little women's club was organized in the sandhills of McPherson County in the western part of Nebraska. The year was 1916. The club was the social life for about one hundred people including all the kids in a radius of fifteen miles. The club met on the first Wednesday of each month.

It took all day for our family to go to Mama's club meeting. We lived at the south end of the area. If Club met at Mrs. Tuckers, who was at the north end, we had fifteen miles to drive our old Ford over roads that were trails made by wagons through the sand and over many hills. There would be at least fifteen barbed wire gates and we had to stop at each one. Someone had to jump out of the car, (always a kid if there was one along that was big enough for the job) run and open the gate, pull it back out of the way. If it was a kid she just climbed over the door getting in and out. It was faster. Our car only had three doors. There was no door for the driver. He was supposed to be a man and climb over. I believe Mama was the only one who used any of the three doors on our Ford. Dad and the kids all climbed over.

Fifteen miles and fifteen gates, it took us over two hours to drive to Mama's club meeting at Tuckers. They had the same thing to go through when Mama entertained.

It was worth it. At noon the hostess served a huge dinner that would compare to any Thanksgiving meal.

After dinner the men headed for the barn and corrals. The kids (usually eight or ten of us) would head out to play, boys and girls together. We played fast and hard. We knew we would not see these kids again until next club day. The women

*A gathering of our family, the Tregos and the Huffmans*

folks, after doing the dishes and cleaning up, went into the living room and started their meeting.

The meeting was very formal and business-like. The roll was called. Each member answered roll call with a verse from the Bible and put her dime (the monthly dues) into the ante pot. The minutes of the previous meeting were read, the current business attended to. The meeting was closed. The women could now discuss the news that they couldn't visit about over the telephone.

This went on until the men came in from the barn and said, "We'd better be heading for home and get the chores done before dark." That was the way it used to be.

As I was preparing to write this story, I had a visit with Helen Petit Mitchell. She was one of the kids that used to go out to play. She married and lived and raised her family on the home ranch left to her by her parents.

Helen's mother was a charter member of the Helping Hand Club, as my mother was. Helen and I were kid members in good standing from the age of four when the club was organized.

Helen is now ninety and living in North Platte in an assisted living home. She has entertained the club twice since moving into Aspen Park. The home prepared and served the dinner. She said the last time she served, ten people attended, six women and four men.

There have been some changes. The dues are now fifty cents a month. The area is much larger. Several of the eighty to ninety-year-old gals have retired from ranch life and moved to either Tryon or North Platte, but still entertain club members when their turn comes up. The distance is twice or three times it was in 1916 and it takes one-fourth the time to make the trip.

I asked Helen if they answered roll call with a verse from the Bible. She told me that now they sometimes have a question to answer. One of the questions, "How old were you when you learned to ride a bicycle?" really made me sit up. I asked her how old she was. Helen said she never could ride a bike.

It brought to my mind what a hard time I had learning to ride. I was fifteen years old before I tried. I was sure there was nothing to it, BUT, I couldn't get on the thing without it falling over. Other kids held it while I got on but as soon as they let go it fell over. I finally got the idea it wasn't a horse I was riding. I couldn't just throw my right leg over, put my foot in the stirrup and have it take off. As soon as I got the idea I had to pedal, riding a bike was fun.

The thought hit me as I was talking with Helen that none of the sandhill kids had a bicycle. Horses were much better in the sand and that is what we all had. Did other kids have trouble transferring from a horse to a bicycle?

Another time the members were to answer roll call telling the first time their husband ever complimented them. I asked Helen if she remembered her husband's first compliment. She answered, "He never did." We chuckled understandably together on that one.

Back to the serious business of the Helping Hand Club of the sandhills. They quietly did much charity work. The ten-cent monthly dues did not bring in much money. They did many worthwhile things to bring in money.

Serving dinners or suppers to large gatherings like at ranch or farm auction sales, brought good income. There were always large crowds at these sales. Some people came to buy; others came to visit. I have been to a few of those sales and they were always fun, plus there was a good meal at noon served by the Helping Hand Club.

The club members took care of the needy. I also remember they sent money to the orphan homes in Omaha and Lincoln.

The ladies worked on many quilts after the meetings were closed, visiting all the while. These quilts were all made by hand, both the piecing and the quilting. The quilts were either sold or raffled off or given as gifts to the needy.

I still have a quilt that was given to my mother, Grace Snyder, in 1927 as a going-away gift when we leased our ranch and moved to town so my sister and I could go to high school. Each member of the club made a nine-inch block of the fan pattern. In her own handwriting she wrote her name, address, age and the family cattle brand on her quilt block. She then embroidered over her handwriting.

The quilt is now seventy-five years old and one of my prized possessions. Each block is still readable. It's fun to look at the blocks and picture the ladies who made them. I am sad when I realize everyone who contributed to that quilt has been dead many, many years.

One block reads Sarah Wagoner, age 90. She put no cattle brand. Everyone called her Grandma Wagoner. She was the grandmother of Helen Petit Mitchell, the lady who helped me with this story. Helen is now the same age that her grandmother was at the time she made the quilt block.

## Chapter Twenty-eight

# THE RUNAWAY WITH THE LUMBER WAGON

There were two beautiful creeks just south of our ranch. Along the banks of these creeks grew much wild fruit. Chokecherries, wild plums and grapes were plentiful if there hadn't been a freeze late in the spring to kill the blossoms. During good years people came from miles around to gather the fruit for their winter supply of jams and jellies.

Down on pretty little Squaw Creek, four miles south of our ranch were chokecherry thickets and wild plum thickets, also wild grapes. Squaw Creek was a busy, crooked fellow, only a mile long. If he ever straightened out he would be about two miles long. Squaw Creek emptied into Birdwood Creek.

The chokecherries ripened in July and were the most sought after. They were also the most work to gather.

It was a bright sunny day in July. We had heard the chokecherries were ripe and plentiful down on Squaw Creek. Mama did not need to rake hay that afternoon. She hitched her faithful rake team, Jake and Geronimo, to the big old lumber wagon. She took seven-year-old Bertie and headed for Squaw Creek to pick fruit.

We had three modes of travel on the ranch, horseback, the old Ford or the lumber wagon. One could not carry the picked fruit home horseback. The old Ford wouldn't travel down by the creek where the fruit was. That left the lumber wagon with Jake and Geronimo.

Mama and Bertie left right after dinner (noon). Bertie felt privileged to be going with Mama. Picking fruit was a fun thing for a kid. I had to stay home and help in the hayfield.

After arriving at the creek, they pulled along the edge until they found a good chokecherry thicket. There they unhitched the horses and tied them to the wagon wheels, got their buckets and went to work.

Bertie picked the cherries near the ground. Mama picked the berries higher up. After Mama had picked the cherries up as high as she could reach, there was still plenty of fruit higher up. She was no good climbing trees, but she could sure climb on a horse, even one wearing only a harness.

Mama untied Geronimo, climbed on the wagon wheel and slid over onto the horse's broad back. She was wearing her old coveralls so she was able to straddle the horse lady-like. (Mama liked doing these things but she wanted them to look lady-like. She was always telling Bertie and me that what we were doing was not lady-like, such as if we were wearing dresses it was not lady-like to let our black sateen bloomers show. To this day both of us cringe if we hear the word lady-like.)

Mama hung a bucket on each hame and rode into the thicket to pick fruit. As she filled her buckets she handed them down to Bertie who emptied them into a big metal tub and handed the buckets back.

Bertie remembers it as an enjoyable afternoon. She was helping Mama pick fruit and was able to talk over things with Mama, no one else demanding her attention.

*Bertie, Nellie and Billie trying to look lady-like. Looks like someone had been busy with the lamp chimney curling iron.*

*Bertie and a cousin not looking very lady-like. The lumber wagon is in the background.*

As I've said before we kids earned our keep from an early age. Bertie continued to pick fruit near the ground even though she had grown tired and slowed a lot. It was nice there in the shade with the running water nearby.

Late in the afternoon Mama noticed the sky darkening in the west. She decided they should quit picking even though the tub was only half full. They hitched the horses back to the wagon, loaded up and headed home.

They had planned to stop at Whites, our neighbor two miles south of our house. The road went within a few feet of the Whites' front door. They hurried the team along. By the time they reached Whites', the cloud was right over them with lightning and thunder.

Mrs. White and her two daughters, Beulah and Nina, were out in the yard to meet them as they drove up to the house. Beulah handed a baby kitten up to Bertie.

The cloud was getting closer and blacker. It was starting to rain. Mama knew they were in trouble. She sat Bertie down on the floor in the corner of the wagon next to where she would be standing braced against the front of the box driving the horses through the storm she knew was upon them.

Mama took her large straw hat off her head and gave it to Bertie. She told Bertie to hold the hat over the kitty so he wouldn't drown.

The Whites ran back into their soddy. Mama started the horses off at a fast trot, still hoping to beat the storm, or as much of it as she could.

The horses's trot became faster and faster until they were loping. Finally they broke into a dead run.

Bertie said the noise was the worst she had ever heard. The big empty seat rattled around on top and the sideboards rattled in their slots. Bertie also says she did not think of herself. She did not realize the danger they were in. Her only concern was keeping the kitty dry and being sure he didn't drown.

Fortunately the horses did not try to leave the road which in places was deep ruts. Had they tried to pull out where the ruts were deep that top heavy lumber wagon could have upset with fatal results. I have read of many such accidents. It was always a man who was killed. This time it would have been a mama and a little girl.

By the time the runaway team reached our level south meadow, it was raining very hard, lots of lightning and thunder, and the horses were still in a dead run. Putting all her weight on the reins, Mama was unable to stop them. She started them circling. That slowed them down.

Each circle brought the team closer to the ranch buildings. Dad and Miles were out there, plenty frightened and ready to do what they could.

Finally Jake and Geronimo were winded enough that Dad and Miles were able to grab their bridles and calm them down. The horses were played out.

Miles held the team while Dad lifted Bertie out of the wagon. She still had the kitten, holding Mama's hat over him even though the rain had stopped.

Mama stayed in the wagon, searching the floor. Her long, waist-length black hair which she always wore pinned on top of her head was stringing down her back, wet from the rain. Her coveralls clung to her body (not so lady-like.)

Dad asked Mama why she didn't get out of the wagon. She told him she had lost all her good hairpins and was hoping to find some of them.

The tub of choke-cherries had bounced all over the floor of the wagon. The tub had not tipped over or spilled any cherries, but the cherries were so smashed down, the jam was half made. We had delicious chokecherry jam that winter.

Another Sandhill delicacy was the sand-cherry. Sand-cherries grew on little bushes close to the ground. They were found in patches in the hills among the pasture grass. Some years they were plentiful and some years there were none.

When Dad and Miles rode the pastures and found a nice patch of sand-cherries that were ripe and ready to pick they would tell Mama where it was.

Mama would round up whomever was available. We saddled up gentle horses. If a kid was too little to saddle her horse, someone saddled it for her. We needed horses that would stand there on three legs and sleep while its rider was off picking berries. We each carried one bucket. The bigger the person, the bigger the bucket.

We headed for the sand-cherry patch. It could be up to two miles from the house. We reached the patch, got off our horses and dropped the reins. The horses were soon asleep. We scattered out and went to work. And work it was. We walked stooped over to pick. And it was hot.

I have a memory of one cherry picking time. We had picked our cherries and were on our way home. There were four of us, Mama, Nellie, Bertie and me.

Bertie was riding old Roany. Roany was the slowest, sweetest kid's horse we had. You put a kid on Roany, tied the reins together and looped them over the saddle horn and he would follow along with the other horses.

Bertie didn't have her own saddle yet. Dad put his big saddle on Roany, lifted little Bertie up in the saddle, hooked the reins over the saddle horn and handed the little bucket up to her. She was ready to ride the two miles out to the sand-cherry patch, holding on to the saddle horn and her bucket, her short legs sticking almost straight out.

It was the ride home that day that leaves the picture in my mind. Each person was carrying her bucket with the sand-cherries she had picked. We were riding at a slow walk. We were all tired. My horse was following Bertie's.

I looked up. Bertie's head was tipped forward. I rode up beside her. Her chin was on her chest and she was sound asleep. Her bucket had tipped over and all of her cherries had spilled out.

We still had sand-cherry jam that winter.

## Chapter Twenty-nine

# MAMA'S COOKBOOK

Mama's recipes are written in pencil in a three-and one-half-by-six inch Moroccan leather bound tally book put out by:

> *Brainard-Carpenter Co.*
> *Live Stock Commission Merchants.*
> *OFFICE 224-226 Exchange Bldg.*
> *Phone: Bell So.70*
> *Established 1887*
> *South Omaha, Nebr.*

Dad shipped cattle to the stockyards in Omaha each fall. He must have received the tally book as a compliment on his shipment of cattle in the fall of 1914. In the back of the book is a calendar for the year 1914.

Whenever Mama got the cookbook out we knew we were going to have something extra special for dinner. Dad's favorite was suet pudding. Brother Miles's favorite was doughnuts. Mama always made a double batch of doughnuts, one batch for Miles and one for the rest of us.

Some of these recipes tell what to put in but not how to do it. Mama knew. Only one recipe gives a baking time. There was no need to give the baking temperature. There was no temperature gauge on the oven. That's another thing Mama just knew.

Many of the recipes have no heading. In other words, sometimes it doesn't tell what you are making.

**Doughnuts**      One cup sour cream

2 eggs

One teaspoon soda

A little nutmeg

One cup sugar

**Chili Sauce**      1 peck tomatoes

9 onions

1 pepper

1 qt. vinegar

2/3 cup salt

1 cup sugar

3 teaspoons of all kinds of spices

## Ice Cream Like You Buy

3 qts of milk

1 qt. of cream

3 cups of sugar

1 ounce of gelatin dissolved in warm milk

the whites of six eggs

Put 1 pt. milk in double boiler and scald, add the gelatin and sugar and pour into the remaining milk, flavor to taste and add the beaten whites of the eggs, last of all, pour in the cream and freeze.

Brother Miles liked ice cream and would happily go to our icehouse and carry up a hunk of ice. He got the one-gallon hand-turned freezer ready, settled in the shade and shaved the ice. He was ready to start freezing by the time Mama had the "Ice Cream Like You Buy" ready to go. Miles always got to lick the ladder or paddle, whatever you call it.

**Cream Puffs**   1 cup hot water

                     1/2 butter boil

                     1 cup level flour

Beat in four eggs one at a time

**Chicken Pie**   2 cups flour

                     1/2 teaspoon salt

                     2 teaspoons Baking Powder

                     2 tablespoons lard

Beat one egg, add to a cup of milk, pour this into flour mixture.

**Vinegar Pie**   1 egg

                     1 tablespoon flour

                     1 cup sugar

                     1 cup cold water

                     2 tablespoons vinegar

                     lemon extract or nutmeg

**Drop Molasses Cookies**

                     1 cup sugar

                     1 cup molasses

                     2/3 cup shortening

                     2 eggs

                     1/4 cup cold water

                     1 teaspoon soda

                     1 teaspoon ginger

                     4 cups flour

Drop by teaspoon on greased tin

**Bread Dough Cake**   (This was my favorite.)

2 scant cups bread dough

1 heaping cup sugar

1/4 cup butter

2 eggs

1 teaspoon soda

1 cup raisins chopped

1 teaspoon of all kinds of spice, 2 of cinnamon

**Candy**      2 cups brown sugar

1/2 cup cream

butter size of walnut

 1 cup nuts

**Spotted Cake**

1 1/4 cup sugar

1 1/2 cups flour

1 teaspoon Baking powder

4 eggs

1 cup cream

flavoring

a little milk

**(No Heading)**

14 cups corn

1 cup sugar

1 cup salt

1 cup hot water

Boil 20 minutes and can.

Sounds like a lot of salt, but that is what it says.

## Tomato Soup Like You Buy

1 peck ripe tomatoes

6 medium onions

celery salt

1 hot red pepper

4 sweet peppers

6 whole cloves

Cook all together until tender. Run thru sieve. Return to the stove and add the following:

1/2 cup butter

salt to taste

1 cup sugar

1 cup flour (mix all these last together)

Stir while cooking until smooth and thick.

## Suet Pudding

1 cup raisins

1 cup chopped raisins

1 cup suet chopped

1/2 cup sorghum

1 tsp soda in hot water

1 egg

spices

flour to make soft batter

1 half cup milk

This next recipe is the one least liked by Bertie and me. We had to take turns stirring it after it was removed from the stove. It didn't taste good either. We knew. We each had had our mouths washed out more than once with the results of this recipe.

**Lye Soap**      2 qts. water

1 can lye

6 lbs. grease

Boil 30 minutes, remove from fire and stir until cold

It took that stuff forever to get cold. We know that, too,because it was our job to take turns stirring it. This was the soap Mama used to wash our mouths out with whenever she heard us say a sin word. This was so we would not go to the Bad Place for having said that word that time.

Come wash day, another job for Bertie and me was to shave a hand-sized cake of that soap to almost powder. This was put in the big boiler on the kitchen range. Mama boiled the white clothes in this before putting them in the old washing machine.

Mama wound up with very white clothes and Bertie and I wound up with very strong hands and clean mouths.

## Chapter Thirty

# THE MORNING THE LIGHTNING STRUCK

This happened July 5th, 1921. I know it was July 5th because the night before was the Fourth of July and the family had enjoyed our fireworks - a few firecrackers and sparklers. I know it was 1921 because Bertie was seven years old.

It was early in the morning and Bertie's turn to wash the breakfast dishes and my turn to dry. Bertie was so little at that time Mama had to put the dishpan on a kitchen chair; another pan was on an adjoining chair. There was warm water and soap in the dishpan and clear warm water in the other pan. Bertie washed the dishes in the soapy water and put them in the warm water pan and I dried them and put them in the cupboard.

The chairs were sitting with their backs to the dining table. That put us between the north and south kitchen doors, which were both wide open. Clearing the table was easy. We just scraped the leftovers into one plate and took them out and gave them to our beloved shepherd dog, Towser. He was always waiting. On mornings we had pancakes Mama made a few extra for Towser. It was fun to throw them at him and watch him catch them. He never missed.

On this particular morning I remember it was very dark as we were doing the dishes. Miles was out on the north porch. He was pumping water. Suddenly there was a loud clap and light was everywhere.

I was over by the cupboard and not between the north and south kitchen doors. I felt nothing but the strangeness of it all.

Little Bertie stood dead still with a table knife in her hand. She had been shocked, but soon came out of it.

Miles came in from the porch and said he had gotten a shock that went from the hand he had on the pump handle down through his body to his feet that were on cement.

Mama came down from upstairs and found her kids alive, but numbed. Soon Dad came in from the barn and said the lightning had scared the night horse we always kept in the barnyard. It happened to be my horse Midget. She was so scared she had run into a wire fence and cut a deep gash in her left shoulder.

We inspected the buildings for more damage. We found the phone wire burned loose from the house. Dad told us kids not to touch the phone wire that was hanging on the ground as it might be charged. I had to know what charged meant and see why I should not touch it. When no one was looking I picked the wire up and wrapped it around my thigh. I found out what charged was. I jumped around and yelled. I wasn't in danger so the whole family laughed at me including Dad, which, of course, really hurt.

My poor horse Midget was the one who suffered. The wire cut was where she could reach it with her mouth. When it started to heal and the itching began, we had to keep her in a stall with her head tied up tight so she couldn't reach the gash with her mouth and tear it wide open.

Midget had to be taken out to the tank twice a day for a drink of water. Once I thought I was big enough to do that job. I untied her to lead her to the tank, but I wasn't strong enough to keep her from chewing her sore leg. Her healing had to start all over again.

Dad told us kids the reason the lightning frightened Midget enough to make her run into the fence was because the fireworks the night before had made her nervous. We had been allowed to set off a few firecrackers and whirl around a sparkler until it died out.

The Fourth of July's on the Snyder ranch were quiet from 1921 to 1927 when we moved to town to go to school.

## Chapter Thirty-one

# FREE SAMPLES

Bertie and I were reminiscing the other day. Bertie said, "Bill, do you remember when we used to send for all those free samples?" We laughed and tried to recall all the things we got.

Sending samples was the method the merchants used to reach outlying areas with their products at that time. All the newspapers and each magazine had coupons with a big "FREE" on them. Anyone who cut out a coupon, wrote her name and address on it and mailed it in received a free sample of whatever was advertised.

Our folks were very conservative or thrifty or whatever you want to call it. Bertie and I weren't allowed to do things that cost much money, such as make out an order to Monkey Wards for toys or useless things. Mama did all the ordering and all we got was clothes.

Each fall after Dad sold the steers, Mama sent off a big order to Monkey Wards for the winter supply of clothes for the whole family. It is still with me how great that fleecy, long-legged underwear felt on cold mornings when it was new.

Each time we asked for toys, Mama\Dad would tell us, "No, they are too expensive," so we waited until the fall catalog came out the next summer. We would grab the big catalog, turn to the toys and ask if they were cheap enough yet. They never were.

What did we need of toys? We each had our own horse and saddle. Kids with lots of toys would have given them all for a horse and saddle.

One toy Dad saw to it we had was a rocking horse, a nice one. He bought one for Nellie and Miles when they were little but I remember riding that little horse many miles.

There was also a sturdy little red wagon bought for Nellie and Miles. We could hitch Buster, our Shetland pony, to the wagon. Fun.

Getting back to the free samples.

We were allowed to send for free samples even though every letter we mailed cost two cents. Mama was postmistress. Her wages for handling the mail twice a week was two and one-fourth cents for each two-cent letter she cancelled and sent to Sutherland with Charlie, the mail carrier. Bertie and I could write all the letters we wanted.

After we got our free sample business going, life was really fun. It was exciting to watch the mails come in to see if one of us received a little package.

I just recall a few of the articles we received. There were tiny tubes of Colgate and Pepsodent toothpaste and little tins of salve. One salve we really liked was called Rosebud. It was a pretty wine color and smelled like rosebuds. We rubbed it on our skin just to smell it. Resinall was the name of another salve. It smelled like the dip they used to treat the cattle for mange. We gave it to the folks to use when they needed salve.

Whenever we received something we didn't know what it was or what it was for, we took it to Mama and asked her. In one mail Bertie received the largest package yet. She really hit the jackpot. She tore it open and out popped a thing about two and one-half inches wide and five inches long, probably one-half inch thick. It was white and nice to hold and felt good when we rubbed it against our faces. But what the heck was it for?

It said "KOTEX" in big letters on the wrapping. We took it to Mama and asked her what it was.

Mama started acting embarrassed and evasive. She kept trying to change the subject. Finally Mama kept that nice soft thing and we left not knowing what it was.

We felt it was another one of those things kids shouldn't know. It was a few years before we understood what Bertie had received.

## Chapter Thirty-Two

# THINGS WE SHOULDN'T

**B**ertie and I were growing old enough to realize some of this stuff Mama and Dad had been telling us just didn't add up at times. The biggie was Santa Claus. We always received something from the folks for Christmas, no matter what, but then there was that very special present from Santa Claus. There was a catch to that one. We had to be really good all year to receive it. "IT" was the best gift and was always store-bought, like the little cowgirl outfit with a cowgirl hat we each received one year.

Bertie and I just could not be even kinda good for very long at one time. We did try and seemed to squeeze by each year. When we finally realized for sure there was no Santa Claus, we talked it over and decided not to let the folks know that we knew. That way we would still receive that extra special gift. We got by with that for a year or two.

Then there was the Easter Bunny. There again if we weren't good the Easter Bunny wouldn't leave us anything. He always brought many pretty colored eggs. Sometimes he even brought candy eggs.

I remember one year there were two big chocolate eggs. I happened to find those two chocolate eggs before Easter came. I was kinda looking for them when I ran onto them.

I couldn't resist taking a bite. I bit the small end off of one of those chocolate eggs. I was one miserable kid until Easter came and I could 'fess up.

We never had chocolate eggs again, but we still had our Easter Egg hunt and the family had our pretty eggs eaten up in a few days.

One year I decided to save some of my eggs. I packed a few of my prettiest eggs in a small box and hid them up in the attic.

It was a few weeks before I thought of my pretty eggs. I went up to take a look.

By now it was summer and hot in the attic. A bad smell came out at me as I opened the little attic door. I went over to my box which was hidden behind the chimney from the cook stove that runs up through the attic. That bad odor was very strong as I reached the box.

I don't recall exactly what the eggs looked like, but they weren't pretty anymore. Now I had to take the mess down and tell the folks what I had done. At least I learned that hard-boiled eggs will rot if kept in a hot room.

Soon I learned the Easter Bunny was just another way of scaring me into being good. So now I knew I didn't have to be good for the Easter Bunny or Santa Claus. I had also realized the stork didn't bring babies. There was one thing that worried me though. It was God. It seems if I told a lie or said enough bad words I would go to the Bad Place. The Bad Place had a big, very hot fire burning in it and it was called hell. I couldn't say "hell" or I would go there and be burned up, so I called it The Bad Place.

Along with the sin words, which were "Hell" and "Damn," were any words referring to our Lord used in the wrong way. If these words were used in a calm voice, that was swearing, but they were still sin words, also known as bad words. When someone said these words in a loud, mad voice, that was cussing and really bad. We only heard cussing from the men as they worked with the horses, cattle and machinery.

If Bertie or I said any bad words we got our mouths washed out with soap. It seemed if Mama washed our mouths out with soap, we might not go to the Bad Place for saying what we had said.

One day Mama was not at home and Bertie said a bad word. There was no one there to wash her mouth out so I told her she had better go out in the kitchen and wash her own mouth out good or she would go to the Bad Place and burn for saying that word.

She did it, but she cried as she rubbed the soap on her tongue. After she finished, we felt sure that now she would not go to the Bad Place.

Mama had taught school a couple of years. She tried to teach her little hellions what she called good grammar. The bad grammar words that Mama really scolded us for using were "ain't," "hain't," "this here," and "that there."

I remember getting a kid's kick out of using the bad grammar words when Mama couldn't hear me. I couldn't let Bertie hear me either or she would tell Mama.

We were turned loose on slang words. Even Mama used the slang words. She used to say, "Dad-blame-it" when things didn't go right, but she always lowered her voice when she said it.

Some of the slang I still use - words like "Doggone," "Gosh darn," and "Blame-it," but to this day neither Bertie or I use any sin words in our conversations.

I started driving a team of horses when I was six years old. Dad hitched a sleepy old team to the cart. It was plenty safe and easy for a small kid to handle, but I felt that I should holler at those gentle old horses just like the men hollered at their more spirited, younger ones.

I used slang words but said them in the same tone of voice that the men used while cussing at their teams. I felt I did a pretty good imitation of a man cussing. I'm wondering now, though, if gentle old Knute and Charlie didn't do a horse chuckle listening to a six-year-old girl's voice trying to talk like a hired man. They had heard all of that and more in their younger years.

As I said before, I found out that all that stuff about Santa Claus, the Easter Bunny and the Stork were just to make kids be good, so then I began to wonder about God. Maybe there was no God. That, too, might be a way to make kids be good. I was kinda hoping that was the case. If so, I would be free to do all the things I wanted to do.

As time went on there was nothing showing to make it look like there was no God. And since I didn't want to take any chances on going to the Bad Place when I died, I still tried to be just as good as it took to keep out of there.

I don't remember thinking of going to heaven, only staying out of that Bad Place.

## Chapter Thirty-three

# WE HEAD WEST

In the spring of 1927 Bertie graduated from the eighth grade. Dad had told us that when Bertie finished grade school he would lease the ranch and show us some of the country and send us to high school. I had graduated in 1925. It was a lonesome two years for me waiting for Bertie to graduate.

Bertie and I could have gone to high school in town, but Mama wasn't about to let her daughters live in town without her. She had to be there to watch over us.

Before we moved, we had a big sale. An auctioneer sold all those things that seemed a part of me.

The saddest of all was when Midget, my fifteen-year-old trick riding horse wearing my old saddle was auctioned off. I rode her into the ring. I managed to hold back the tears until the bidding was over.

*Billie on Midget.*

As soon as I knew she was sold (she brought forty dollars, and that included saddle, saddle blanket and bridle), I got off, dropped the reins and ran through the crowd of people to the house. I was crying pretty good by then.

I never saw Midget again.

After the sale we still had to have a dance - that was customary in those days for any family leaving the Sandhills. All a Sandhill dance needed for music was a fiddle or two and there were two or three neighbors who were good fiddlers. The only things left in the house were the kitchen range in the kitchen and the heating stove in the living room. The stove in the living room was taken out to make more room. The stove was taken out every summer anyway.

There were a lot of good-byes said that night. We did not see those people again for over four years.

After the sale and the big dance, Dad loaded the family into two Fords. One Ford was a 1926 black touring car, the kind with curtains. It was a big job to fasten the curtains on and it was only done in real cold weather or when it rained very hard.

The other Ford was a 1920 model. We called this the old car or the truck. Dad cut the back of the body off of it and built on a tall frame rack. In the rack Dad loaded three tents, one for Mama and Dad, one for Miles, one for we three girls, and four bedrolls. There was one double bedroll for Dad and Mama and one double bedroll for Bertie and me. Nellie and Miles each had a single bedroll. The single bedrolls were half the width of the double bedrolls and took up less room in the rack.

Each bed was made and rolled up in heavy canvas and fastened with a leather strap and buckle. When the bed was laid on the ground and unrolled, the bedding was protected from dampness by the canvas. The top layer of canvas was rolled back to the foot of the bed and there was a nicely made bed - sheets, quilts and all.

Oftentimes Bertie and I wanted to sleep in the open under the stars. The folks would let us unroll our bed just outside their tent. We were safe there and if it happened to rain before morning Dad would get up and pull the canvas tarp up over our heads. We liked to listen to the rain on the tarp. I think we slept out in the open more than we did in the tent.

The rack also held the rest of our camping gear and a two-burner gas camp stove, the kind Mama had to pump up before she could light it. There were two iron skillets, a couple of pots and enough dishes for all of us. That rack was packed with everything needed for six people to camp all summer.

Dad also built a cupboard that fit the back of the box he had built on the "truck." He fashioned the cupboard after the old grub boxes on the mess wagons they used on the roundups in his cowboy days. The front of the cupboard or grub box was hinged at the bottom and fastened shut at the top. There was a substantial leg hinged in the center at the top. The front of the grub box opened up and using the leg for support made a nice workbench for the cook. Mama adapted very well to mess wagon cooking and we all had a wonderful time that summer.

The trip made me forget my two years of loneliness. It was late May 1927 when we left and headed west not knowing where we would stop to live for the next four years.

I think we were all hoping we would make it to the Pacific Ocean. We sure wanted to see the ocean. The family pastime that winter had been pouring over road maps.

We found Salem, Oregon on the map and that wasn't very far from the ocean. Dad had a sister living there. We had never seen her but all of a sudden we wanted to get acquainted with Aunt Alice.

The roads, even the main highways, were only graded and graveled. There was very little pavement - no pavement through the Rocky Mountains or any other ranges of mountains. The roads were only wide enough for two lanes of traffic, one going each way. Those roads looked good to us. We were used to two trails in the sand making one road. In the sandhills the rule was when two cars met, each car pulled his right wheels out of one rut keeping his left wheel in his legal rut. Thus the two cars safely passed.

If one car got stuck in the sand, the driver of the other vehicle, man or woman, helped to push him or her out. No road rage in the good old days. The two drivers would, of course, stop as they passed and discuss something of interest to both of them. I never remember a head-on collision when we used sand trails for highways.

On these new roads we stayed on our side and the other driver stayed on his side–unless he was road hogging. We tried very hard not to be road hogs, even going through the Rocky Mountains where the roads were narrow with many S curves.

Going around those curves when we were in the outside lane was very scary. We all caught ourselves leaning to the inside as we rode the mountains.

We tried hard not to break any rules. We were out of our territory (the Sandhills) and life was different, but so exciting. We were traveling west by way of the Black Hills of South Dakota and northern Wyoming.

I might put in here that our dad was Pinnacle Jake of the book, "Pinnacle Jake," written by my sister, Nellie Snyder Yost. It was first published in 1953 and is still in print.

On this trip Dad retraced his old cowboy days as well as looked the country over for better ranching country. He thought the Sandhills were getting too fenced in. As it turned out, five years later he was happy to get back on his ranch in the Sandhills.

Our first night away from the ranch was spent at Grandma Wilson's just north of Sutherland. Grandma Wilson was Mrs. Nate Trego's mother. The Nate Tregos were our good friends and neighbors six miles west of our ranch. The Trego family also spent the night there, giving us a big sendoff.

The next morning we loaded up and headed north for the Black Hills. Miles drove the truck and I rode with him. We led the caravan or broke trail, as Dad said. Dad, Mama, Nellie and Bertie followed in the touring car with Mama and Dad changing as drivers. Dad did not like to drive; he wanted to look at the country. Mama drove most of the time. That was the way we traveled all the way to the Pacific Ocean.

One of our first nights of camping was in the Chadron State Park. There Dad started teaching us kids how to camp. He showed us how to pitch our tent and how to place our bedroll and unroll it. He taught us more later on in the trip.

Our next stop was Hot Springs, South Dakota. Our average rate of speed from Sutherland to the Pacific Ocean must have been from twenty to thirty miles an hour. I don't recall passing another car on the trip.

*A Sandhill swimming party.*
*Billie on the left and Bertie*
*and Mama on the right.*

The only picture I have in mind of Hot Springs is the Evans Plunge, a big closed-in, warm water swimming pool - the most wonderful place I'd ever seen. We had dog-paddled in the meadow lakes at home wearing old clothes, maybe even heavy denim overalls.

We couldn't swim but now we had real bathing suits even though the skirts came almost to our knees. We felt so with it. I made up my mind there that as soon as we stopped for the winter, the first thing I would do would be learn to swim by taking real swimming lessons and I did.

The next stop was Mount Rushmore. We had heard they were going to carve President Washington's face on the side of Mount Rushmore. We sure wanted to see that. We drove out to the mountain but the men had only started chiseling on the side of the mountain. We saw them working up there, but nothing looked like George Washington's face.

It was three years later before the first president's face was completed, with three more presidents' faces following. Each member of our family has been back to see the finished project. I wonder if like me, the others looked at the wonderment and thought back to 1927 and what the sight was in the first stages.

We left Mount Rushmore and drove up to Rapid City. The story we had been hearing while in the Black Hills was that President Coolidge was going to Rapid City to spend the summer. I was hoping to get to see him. I wanted to tell him we had heard in the Sandhills that his son had died from an infected blister on his heel. If that was so, I wanted to tell him I was very sorry.

We did not see hide nor hair of President Coolidge.

We were in the country where Dad had spent much of his cowboy days and there were places he wanted to see. We spent several days visiting Dead Wood, Belle Fourche and Spearfish in South Dakota, Moorcroft, The Devils Tower and many other places in Wyoming.

We spent a lot of time in Wyoming. The thing I remember most vividly is that campgrounds were scarce and Wyoming was where Dad taught us more about camping.

When we came across a nice stream, we camped there. It didn't matter what time of day it was, we stopped and set up camp. Dad showed us that in selecting a good campsite we had to find ground that sloped enough to let the water run off if it rained.

Gas stations were very different then than now. Mostly they were small and junky, usually having only one gas pump. The gas pumps were always red with a glass top. The tops were measured in gallons. Thus we could see how much gas they put in our car. The glass top had to be refilled by pushing a lever on the side back and forth by hand, which was fine since there were no other cars waiting. The gas attendant had plenty of time.

There were homemade signs along the side of the road telling how far to the next station and what it had to offer. The signs all said "gas and oil" unless there was a restroom available. Not all stations had them. Restroom was a new word to us and Mama said it in the same hushed tone she used for saying privy.

We kids were very excited on reaching Cody, Wyoming, the entrance to Yellowstone Park. We had read of Old Faithful Geyser and heard of bears and other animals in the Park. Dad had a great interest in the grizzly bears. We had heard him talk of the "Grizzly" many times as he told us stories of his old cowboy days in Wyoming while we crossed the state where a lot of the stories took place.

Dad could make any trip interesting with his stories. If he hadn't been there he had read the history - which brings to mind a trip Dad, Mama, Bertie and I took in the summer of 1930.

We drove from Salem, Oregon to San Diego, California to visit Mama's mother.

As we rode along Dad would say, "It was about in here that a certain thing happened." Then he would tell an interesting story, a story which interested even an eighteen-year-old kid like me with other things on her mind.

Oh yes. We were just entering Yellowstone Park. The first thing to impress me was the beautiful log cabin hotel, Old Faithful Lodge. A big group of geysers could be seen from the hotel. People were headed toward the geyser and we followed. We heard someone say that Old Faithful was due to erupt. We waited a few minutes then stood there with our mouths open as we watched that beautiful geyser shoot high up in the air. We came back many times during our stay in the park to watch it happen again.

Only very rich people stayed in the lodge. The rest of us camped in tents. We camped on the shore of Yellowstone Lake, a wonderful spot - at least Dad thought so. We stayed there three

*Old Faithful Geyser in Yellowstone Park, 1927*

weeks. We must have all been very healthy when we left as we had lived on salmon trout the whole time.

We saw plenty of bears while camped there. We also heard them at night as they came into camp looking for food. We shared our food with the bears a few times.

I have no record of when we arrived at the Park or when we left. We were there on the Fourth of July. It snowed that day and was very cold.

Mama, Miles, Bertie and I had taken our fishing gear and started to fish in Yellowstone River, moving up the river as we fished. It was cloudy and cold, but we caught fish and it was fun.

When it started to snow we agreed to give up and head back to camp. All but Miles. He wanted to go on up the river fishing.

Mama, Bertie and I started back to camp carrying a long, heavy string of fish. The fish were strung on a rope by the gills. Two of us carried it changing off. We all remember the Fourth of July in Yellowstone Park in 1927.

One other story I remember in Yellowstone Park happened the cold morning we loaded up to leave. Both of our Fords had to be cranked to start. Miles always cranked the truck and Dad cranked the touring car. That morning Dad had a kink in his back and couldn't bend over. Miles had an infected finger on his right hand. His hand was badly swollen.

I was always trying to show off my strength and told the folks I could turn the crank enough times to get both cars started. I also had in mind that if I could get the cars started surely Dad would let me drive one. I'd been begging him from the time we left home to let me drive.

It was cold that morning and it took a lot of cranking but I got both cars started. I know I grew several inches while turning that crank. I went back to size fast when Dad told me I still couldn't drive. Miles drove our truck. Mama drove the new car.

There was a little town outside the Park called West Yellowstone. There we found a doctor for Miles. We all went into the doctor's office with him. I learned what fainting might feel like as I watched the doctor lance Miles's hand.

We all left the doctor's office, got back in our cars and Miles drove with a wrapped up hand. There was a good feeling all around for we knew we were headed for the ocean.

As we came into Oregon, we drove along the Columbia River. We felt that this was where we wanted to live.

Seeing the Pacific Ocean was a thrill for all of us. I'm sure everyone had goose bumps, the same as I.

We pitched our tents and made camp as close to the ocean as we could. We spent the day exploring the beach, watching the horizon for anything that might show up out there. We kids got our feet wet in the Pacific Ocean. I couldn't wait to write to friends back home and tell 'em that one.

We went to sleep that night listening to the noise the waves made. As I awakened the next morning and heard the same noise my heart felt heavy. I thought that sound was Nebraska wind and I was supposed to get up and go pick up cowchips. Then I realized I had picked up my last cowchip.

*Some Ten Bar White Face herefords. That's Mama sitting on the back corral fence. Not only the kids used the corrral fence for a grandstand seat.*

*Moving in the Sandhills. Some people took their house with them—saved packing.*

*A common Sunday at a Sandhill lake. The fish better take care—these kids know how to fish.*

 **ORDER FORM**

for additional copies of

## BERTIE and ME
### Growing Up on a Nebraska Sandhill Ranch
### in the Early 1900's
By Billie Lee Snyder Thornburg

**Fax orders:** 308-532-1748 – *Send this form.*
**Telephone orders:** Call 308-532-1748
**Email orders:** billielee@inebraska.com
**Postal orders:** The Old Hundred and One Press
2220 Leota Street
North Platte, NE 69101

**Shipping by air:**

*U.S.: $ ____ shipping for the first book and $ ____ for each additional book.*
*International: $ ____ shipping for the first book and $ ____ for each additional book.*

*Please send me _____ copies of* **BERTIE and Me** *@ $18.95 each plus shipping.*
*TOTAL ENCLOSED: _____*

*Name:_____*

*Address:_____*

*City, State, ZIP: _____*